THE
ABCs
OF Success

THE ABCs OF Success

The Essential Principles from
America's Greatest Prosperity Teacher

BOB PROCTOR

JEREMY P. TARCHER/PENGUIN

an imprint of Penguin Random House

New York

Jeremy P. Tarcher/Penguin
An imprint of Penguin Random House LLC
375 Hudson Street
New York, New York 10014

Copyright © 2015 by Proctor Gallagher Institute
Penguin supports copyright. Copyright fuels creativity, encourages diverse voices,
promotes free speech, and creates a vibrant culture. Thank you for buying an authorized
edition of this book and for complying with copyright laws by not reproducing, scanning,
or distributing any part of it in any form without permission. You are supporting writers
and allowing Penguin to continue to publish books for every reader.

Most Tarcher/Penguin books are available at special quantity discounts for bulk purchase
for sales promotions, premiums, fund-raising, and educational needs. Special books
or book excerpts also can be created to fit specific needs. For details,
write: SpecialMarkets@penguinrandomhouse.com.

Library of Congress Cataloging-in-Publication Data

Proctor, Bob.
The ABCs of success : the essential principles from
America's greatest prosperity teacher / Bob Proctor.
p.   cm.
ISBN 978-0-399-17518-3 (paperback)
1. Success in business.   2. Success.   I. Title.
HF5386.P87   2015   2015001026
650.1—dc23

Printed in the United States of America
5   7   9   10   8   6   4

Book design by Ellen Cipriano

While the author has made best efforts to determine the source of all quotes
contained herein, when a quote is commonly attributed to two people,
the author has not included a definitive source.

This publication is designed to provide accurate and authoritative information
in regard to the subject matter covered. It is sold with the understanding that
the publisher is not engaged in rendering legal, accounting, or other professional
services. If you require legal advice or other expert assistance, you should seek
the services of a competent professional.

To our dedicated team at the Proctor Gallagher Institute, the team that has taken us into over one hundred countries, and helped to positively impact millions of lives, I am forever grateful.

Foreword

In 2006, at a seminar in Vancouver, Washington, a man I'd never met, seen, or heard of before stepped onto a stage in front of me, began speaking, and proceeded to change the course of my life forever.

That man's name was Bob Proctor. And the day I spent in his audience all those years ago, soaking up his energy and wisdom and jotting down notes like crazy, marked the beginning of a journey I had never imagined myself taking, toward a future I had never envisioned—though I came to realize it was the future I had been destined for all along.

As I would quickly learn, I wasn't the only one who'd had such an experience after meeting him. In fact, I was one of millions.

But Bob Proctor didn't just help facilitate my new future; he became an essential part of it. You see, I made a sudden and absolute decision at that seminar: I decided that one day, I was going to work with this incredible man. Not just work with him, but become a member of his inner circle of advisers.

Soon after that seminar, I walked away from a thriving law practice and booming, lucrative career to do exactly that. I have never looked back.

Today, as his business partner, his collaborator, and—the role I most cherish—his friend, I am reminded on a day-to-day, sometimes minute-to-minute basis, of exactly why Bob Proctor is one of the most respected, listened-to, and beloved people on this planet.

"How does he do it?" Walk through the crowd at a Bob Proctor event (and there's always a crowd) and you'll hear that question a lot. How does he have so much energy? How does he manage to do so much, to connect with so many, to always seem as excited and passionate about the information he's presenting as if he has just discovered it for the first time?

Having now spent countless hours with him, I can tell you that there's no "seem" about Bob's passion or belief. It's 100 percent real, every time.

Everything Bob does comes from a place of absolute genuineness, conviction, and generosity. He is a living testament to the truth and effectiveness of everything he teaches. He knows, from the most powerful, indelible sort of personal experience, that with the right combination of faith, knowledge, and action, anything—*anything*—is possible, for anyone. He is consistently awed by the magnificence of this truth, and he's on a mission, in every moment of his life, to awaken as many people to it as he possibly can.

And if it also "seems" as if he's plugged in to some sort of cosmic energy source in pursuit of this mission, he'll be the first one to tell you that he absolutely is . . . and that there's an open outlet for anyone who wants to join him!

Yet there remains something about Bob Proctor that defies definition or categorization—something that can't be explained by his past, his experiences, or his accomplishments; something remarkably rare and precious. Many know the truth. Many live the truth. But very few are able to make the truth known and livable to others. He IS. As one gentleman at a recent event so perfectly put it, "You could hear the same thing a hundred times from a hundred great people. But somehow, when Bob says it, you get it. You *believe* it."

Of the many wonderful gifts he possesses, I believe this one is his greatest. Truly, there is no one else in the world quite like Bob Proctor.

The writings we've brought together in this collection represent Bob at his very best. As you read them, you'll witness his amazing ability to distill the most complex questions and challenging concepts down to something simple, clear, and completely understandable: his extraordinary gift for seeing and articulating the profundity in ordinary occurrences and the magic in everyday moments, and his uncanny knack for saying exactly the right thing, at precisely the right moment and in just the right way, to flip the switch . . . to make it all suddenly click.

This is what Bob Proctor did and continues to do for me. It's what he has done for so, so many people all over the world. It's what he will do for you, too, the moment you let him into your life.

Turn the page, and start right now. I promise . . . you'll LOVE where it leads you.

—Sandra Gallagher, President,
CEO, and Cofounder,
Proctor Gallagher Institute

Whidbey Island, Washington
May 2014

This book has been created from radio shows that Bob conducted for a number of years. Scripts were selected and edited for the purposes of the book by Sandy Gallagher, Gina Hayden, Cory Kelly, and Shelia Lothian.

Contents

ACHIEVEMENT

Straight As

In school, straight As were always indicative of a great year.

In business, the same rule applies:

Straight As will give you what you want every time. With Awareness, Acceptance, and Alteration comes Achievement.

First, you must become Aware of the primary cause of the results you are getting. The truth is not always in the appearance of things. Your results are never caused by something outside of yourself; results are always an inside job. Your results are a physical or outward expression of the inner conditioning in your subconscious mind.

Your behavior is causing your results . . . and your conditioning is causing your behavior.

The second A is Acceptance. You must accept responsibility for your results. When you accept full responsibility for your own results, you will make the necessary decisions to alter them.

Acceptance of this truth is always the preamble to a magnificent future.

When you accept your subconscious conditioning as the cause of your results, you will be ready for the third A—Alteration. You will decide to alter the conditioning in your subconscious mind, conditioning that is both genetic and environmental. You and your results are actually the product of someone else's habitual way of thinking. To make the necessary alterations in this area not only takes time, it takes a respectable amount of study and discipline, but it's worth it.

It is well worth every penny and every speck of energy you invest in learning how to alter your old conditioning.

This simple process will permit you to ACHIEVE whatever goal you set.

Let's review it. Become Aware of the cause of your results. Accept responsibility for your results. Alter your conditioned subconscious mind. Achieve any goal you set.

Straight As—aim for them!

Nothing stops the man who desires to achieve.
Every obstacle is simply a course to develop his
achievement muscle. It's a strengthening
of his powers of accomplishment.

I attempt an arduous task; but there is no worth in
that which is not a difficult achievement.

ACTION

The Devil's Most Prized Possession

The personal association I had with Earl Nightingale was a great education, but I could never estimate the effect his recorded messages have had on my life.

One of those messages was titled "That's Good." I listened to it so often, I could almost repeat it verbatim. On that record, he shared a fable about the devil having a sale that is most interesting. Like most old fables, it has a moral well worth thinking about.

The story goes that Satan was having a sale of his wares. There on display, and offered for sale, were the rapier of jealousy, the dagger of fear, and the strangling noose of hatred, each with its own high price.

But standing alone on a purple pedestal was a worn and battered wedge. This was the devil's most prized possession, for with it alone he could stay in business. It was not for sale. It was the wedge of discouragement.

Why do you suppose the devil valued so highly, and actually

would not sell, the worn and battered wedge of discouragement? Makes you think, doesn't it?

He prized discouragement because of its enfeebling, demoralizing effect. Hatred, fear, or jealousy may lead immature people to act unwisely, to fight, or to run. But at least they act.

Discouragement, on the other hand, hurts people more than any of these. It causes them to sit down, pity themselves, and do nothing.

Now, this doesn't have to happen.

Unfortunately, it all too frequently does. Not until we realize that discouragement is often a form of self-pity do we begin to take stock of ourselves and our predicament and decide to act . . . to do something that will take us out of the unpleasant situation.

The answer to discouragement, then, is intelligent action. Get rid of discouragement before it gets rid of you. The devil might not survive without this priceless wedge, but you can.

There are risks and costs to action. But they are far less
than the long-range risks of comfortable inaction.

Action is a great restorer and builder of confidence. Inaction
is not only the result, but the cause, of fear.
Perhaps the action you take will be successful; perhaps
different action or adjustments will have to follow.
But any action is better than no action at all.

Doubt, of whatever kind, can be ended by action alone.

Thought Plus Action

Successful living consists of knowing and being. When the two are separated, there is nothing but frustration and failure.

To know all about love without loving can be disastrous. In the same way, knowing all about the right way to live and not acting on what you know, on a daily basis, can prove to be very destructive for anyone.

Unfortunately, most of the self-help books on our bestseller lists deal with positive thinking, without much concern for translating it consciously into experience. We are supplied with maps to Nirvana but cannot locate the vehicle to get us there.

If positive thinking alone resulted in successful living, 95 percent of our population would reside on Easy Street. All of our preachers and teachers would be physical examples of health, wealth, and well-being. Unfortunately, many are physical contradictions to what they tell us.

Half-truths are more elusive than lies. Positive thinking as a medium to the good life is just that: a half-truth.

Positive thinking alone does not deliver, it does not fulfill. In fact, it frustrates, because it is not in harmony with what we do. Thinking positively about music will not make you a musician. Only singing and playing a musical instrument will bring you fulfillment.

The power of positive thought lies in its being expressed in a positive act. The thought of love finds its fulfillment in loving. Thoughts of joy find their power in laughter. Faith without action is dead.

Nothing can result so negatively as thinking positively without the action that fulfills that thinking.

Schools should award diplomas for what we do rather than what we know. Nothing is more powerful than a positive thought joined with positive action.

The ancestor of every action is a thought.

Follow effective action with quiet reflection. From the quiet reflection will come even more effective action.

Action is the real measure of intelligence.

Wake Up

Winners are wide awake; they are alive. Every day you will find them in the marketplace making things happen. The real winners are not just dreamers. Although they have dreams, they are doers: They realize their dreams. They are the bell ringers, always attempting to wake others up to the numerous opportunities life offers.

If you want to cash in on the rewards life has to offer, follow the winners. Do as they do, and ultimately you will become the winner you are capable of being.

If you are not presently living the way you really want to live, don't feel bad about it or have any regrets about the past. Today can be the beginning of a new life. Just as you turn the page on the calendar to reveal a new day or month, mentally you can do that with your life.

Listen to the winners. They want to help you. Every day they are offering you membership in their club.

The greatest reward a winner can receive is to see someone who has been in a deep psychological sleep wake up and grab that brass ring. The winners are openly rewarded for the help they provide.

They are easy to spot; they very rarely hide. They drive nice vehicles, wear good clothes, live in beautiful homes, take interesting vacations, have happy families, and live in healthy bodies. They have dynamic, creative personalities and are almost always involved in executing a big idea.

Winners do not permit the criticism of the losers to distract or slow them down.

They are too busy turning their dreams into reality and helping others do the same thing.

. . . .

Winning is not a sometime thing; it's an all the time thing.
You don't win once in a while, you don't do things
right once in a while, you do them right all the time.
Winning is habit. Unfortunately, so is losing.

When it is obvious that the goals cannot be reached,
don't adjust the goals, adjust the action steps.

Do you want to know who you are? Don't ask. Act!
Action will delineate and define you.

. . . .

AMBITION

You're a Natural

*Do you ever think of yourself as a natural goal achiever?
If you don't, you should, because you are . . . a natural
goal achiever.*

The moment the first breath of life filled your lungs you set out pursuing goals. You are innately programmed to improve the quality of your life. Each of your first early achievements brought with them tremendous satisfaction, along with great pride and joy.

Your first goal was to get something to eat, and when have you ever seen anyone more satisfied than a baby who has just been fed? Or where have you seen greater pride and joy than on the face of a new mother nursing her baby?

How about those other first early goals—to crawl, to talk, or to walk? Think of the satisfaction, pride, and joy that came with that first word or first step. The satisfaction with the first word or step soon wears off and dissatisfaction sets in. You want to put words together, steps together. They became goals and as you accomplished them, more satisfaction, pride, and joy followed, but so did the feeling of dissatisfaction. You wanted to accomplish more, do greater things.

You naturally want to experience life and experience it in abundance. You not only should, you can have the things you want—all of them—and you will have them if you rekindle that early spirit that caused you to pursue and achieve those first goals.

Unfortunately, too many of us were told at an early stage that we should be satisfied with what we had. Goals and their importance were lost.

You should never be satisfied. Happy, but not satisfied. Dissatisfaction is a creative state. It took you out of the cave and put you into the condominium. It gave you the wheel, the fax, and the furnace. Dissatisfaction gave you and me a lifestyle that is the envy of the world.

Develop a healthy dissatisfaction with your life. Set new goals—big, exciting goals. Then, set out to achieve them with the same enthusiasm you knew and used as a baby.

That is called living. Everything else is dying.

. . . .

Big results require big ambitions.

Aim high. Behave honorably. Prepare to be alone
at times, and to endure failure. Persist!
The world needs all you can give.

To strive, to seek, to find, and not to yield.

—ALFRED LORD TENNYSON

. . . .

ATTITUDE

Our Gift

Nature gave a wonderful gift to most of her little creatures—a gift we call "protective coloring"—so that the deer blends into the forest, the fish into the stream, and the bird into the tree. But from one notable creature was this gift withheld. The human creature stands out like a sore thumb on any sort of terrain.

I believe this is because the human was given a much greater gift: You and I have the godlike power to make our surroundings change to fit us.

When you change or improve as a person, your environment and surroundings change to reflect this improvement. Just as you can tell what a business is doing for a community by observing what the community is doing for the business, so can you, with a few notable exceptions, tell what a person is doing for the community by assessing what the community has done for the person.

You can tell a lot about a person by carefully examining his or her environment. Contrary to popular belief, people are not the reflection of their environment nearly as much as we might think. Environment is a reflection of the people. Change the people for the better, and the environment will change for the better as well.

Watch one person change, and that person will leave his or her old environment and seek out a new one—one that more closely reflects their emerging being.

Our attitude is the environment we carry with us during the day. It proclaims to the world what we think of ourselves and indicates the sort of person we have made up our minds to be.

It is the person we will become.

Yes, as we look at the fish, the bird, or the animals in the wild, we do marvel at how well nature has camouflaged them. But don't you think we should spend a little time being overwhelmed by our great gift of creative ability . . . then do all we can to develop and utilize this ability?

Our environment, the world in which we live and work,
is a mirror of our attitudes and expectations.

Your living is determined not so much by what life
brings to you as by the attitude you bring to life;
not so much by what happens to you as by
the way your mind looks at what happens.

Right

"That's right." "It's right." "He's right." "She's right."
Those words are echoed every day by millions of people.
Once we decide we are right, an abundance of energy
goes into defending our rightness.

However, if we look at the situation objectively, we
will quickly become aware that we are never right.

Our way may be a good way. It can be a valid way. It might even be a better way. But it will never be the "right" way. The minute you believe your way is the right way, all other ways will be wrong. That attitude will quickly paralyze progress and shut down the creative juices.

Permit me to make a suggestion.

The next time you hear yourself saying, "That's right," or, "I'm right," correct yourself immediately by repeating, "That is a good way, and I might act on it. However, there is a better way, and I will look for it."

The first telephones were a good way, a better way, even a great way to communicate. However, history has proven that the first telephones were certainly not the best way to communicate. By comparison with today's telephone systems, they were terrible.

This basic concept holds true with everything we do, from

health care to air travel. Think of your own business or industry and the role you play in it. You could very easily be caught in the trap of doing your job the same way because you believe it is the right way. It may be effective . . . but there is always a better way. One small adjustment could improve your productivity 100 percent.

Your way may be effective, it may be valid, but it's never right. There is a better way. Find it!

. . . .

Our attitude toward others determines
their attitude toward us.

No amount of experimentation can ever prove me right;
a single experiment can prove me wrong.

Honest disagreement is often a good sign of progress.

. . . .

Rise Above It

One of the most common reactions to frustration is aggression. Let someone drive in front of us and block our progress while we are rushing to an appointment, and our thin veneer of civilized behavior peels off with a blast on the horn or an angry shout.

While aggression may be a direct and common reaction to frustration, the reaction itself often leads to additional sources of frustration, especially if it is another person who is the target of the aggression. The other person may hit back.

Showing our anger at a police officer who pulls us over for not coming to a full stop may change the officer's decision from giving us a warning to giving us a ticket with a fine.

Psychologists used to think that frustration automatically leads to aggression. Further research suggested that that was not true in all people or all cultures. If aggression is a learned response, it can be unlearned and other more adaptive responses substituted.

Sir Alec Guinness, the great actor of stage and screen, suggested an excellent substitute. Guinness told a story of how his friend and fellow actor Sir Tyrone Guthrie had a phrase for everything that went wrong. Guinness said Guthrie used this phrase for everything from a toothache to a catastrophe, such as the loss of the company's costumes when they were on the road.

It was just three simple words: "Rise above it."

I'm sure you will agree, if we all faced our troubles in that frame of mind, many of those troubles would vanish, and the frustration that often accompanies our problems would disappear.

Put it to the test today with the first problem you are faced with. Just say, "Rise above it." Repeat it aloud: "Rise above it."

. . . .

Nothing can stop the man with the right mental attitude
from achieving his goal; nothing on earth can help
the man with the wrong mental attitude.

Everything can be taken from a man but one thing: the last
of human freedoms—to choose one's attitude in any
given set of circumstances, to choose one's own way.

—VIKTOR FRANKL

. . . .

Awareness

Room of Mirrors

The other day I was speaking with a dear friend who was sharing her situation with me. It wasn't exactly pleasant. Her husband was very unhappy, critical of everyone and most everything. He didn't want to go anywhere or do anything.

She explained, "He acts as if everyone and everything is against him."

The lady's description of her husband reminds me of something that I read years ago about the person whose mind was like a room with mirrored walls. It wouldn't matter which way he looked, all he was ever able to see was himself and his situation.

He would not be able to invoke the law of relativity. Not being able to compare his life with most of the world's population, he would never know, by comparison, that he was living much like Solomon in all his splendor and glory.

Actually, this man's down-and-out attitude was caused by thinking only of himself. Most, if not all, of his problems would be solved if he replaced the mirrored walls of his mind with windows. Then he would see what an absolutely fascinating world we live in—full of color, interesting people, and opportunity. There would be so many challenging things to do and places to go that he would forever be scrambling for time.

When an individual is super sensitive, jumps at conclusions, and allows themselves to be negative, they are showing their immaturity.

By replacing the mirrors with windows, this high level of sensitivity can be converted into awareness, and negative impressions made to serve as a stimulus for creative thought.

This, in turn, will lead to happiness, peace of mind, and a fulfilled life.

. . . .

The greatest discovery of my generation is that a person can change his future by merely changing his attitude.

In order to carry a positive action, we must develop here a positive vision.

To be conscious means not simply to be, but to be reported, known, to have awareness of one's being added to that being.

. . . .

CHANGE

Leave the Cage

What is it in your life you would most like to change? Think of this . . . the starting point of all change is when we change the dominant beliefs that have been limiting our awareness.

William James pointed out that change begins with changing the inner aspects of our thinking. I have learned from experience that an outward change will come after we change from within. By changing some of our most cherished beliefs, we change our awareness and, hence, our reactions to people, circumstances, and conditions.

For centuries, the masses of people have passed along from one generation to the next the false belief that some people have greater potential than others. This false belief has caused many individuals to live like a bird in a cage, which has no idea of how much vast space exists outside. Their mistaken certainties have prevented them from realizing how truly worthy, capable, and unique they are.

These poor misguided souls give credence to the old German proverb that states, "An old error is always more popular than a new truth."

The truth is, you can change whatever it is in your life you would like to change. Life can and should be an exciting adventure. If you are planning to get more out of life in the future than you have in the past, change is essential.

You cannot get improved results in your life with the same old behavior.

The beautiful truth about change with respect to results is that one small change in your actions often produces a tremendous change in your results. You have the potential to change, to take charge of your life, and to really live.

Do it now!

. . . .

Free the child's potential, and you will
transform him into the world.

Some painters transform the sun into a yellow spot,
others transform a yellow spot into the sun.

. . . .

CHOICE

Only You Can Decide

Every day, governments in one place or another are introducing pieces of legislature, enacting new laws, making more rules in an attempt to make their people more successful and happier individuals.

Permit me to share something Theodore Roosevelt wrote many years ago on this subject.

There has never been devised, and there never will be devised, any law which will enable a person to succeed save by the exercise of those qualities which have always been the prerequisite of success: hard work, keen intelligence and unflinching will.

It is foolish for anyone to sit back waiting to see what the government is going to do for us. I am not suggesting governments don't make a difference . . . they do . . . many times, a big difference. But there are many things a government cannot do for us.

There are those things only we can do for ourselves.

For instance, only you can decide to do good work, to give everything you've got to what you do, to be your very best.

Only you can decide to use your intelligence . . . to think . . . to think positive, progressive, constructive thoughts and then govern your life according to those thoughts.

Don't let yourself be swayed by the opinions of others, by the chatter of the masses. Only you can decide to develop an unflinching will, to concentrate, to stay focused on your chosen objective until the task is successfully completed.

By following Theodore Roosevelt's advice, you can most certainly be happy and successful, possibly beyond your wildest dreams.

When Werner von Braun was asked what it would take to send a rocket to the moon, he answered, "The will to do it." That advice will get you to any destination you choose. Happiness and success are gifts you give yourself.

. . . .

Change your life today. Don't gamble on
the future, act now, without delay.

It is in vain to expect our prayers to be heard,
if we do not strive as well as pray.

. . . .

Problems Are Mental in Nature

In Raymond Holliwell's book Working with the Law, *the author suggests that our problems are mental in nature. They have no existence outside of themselves, and it has been discovered that nearly all will yield up their solutions when subjected to a broad and exact analysis.*

Holliwell went on to suggest that you and I should have good and sound reasons for all of the views we hold. As we try to find these, many of our old-time views will fall to pieces. We should form clear and definite ideas regarding our convictions as to why we do as we do and as to why we think as we think.

That is excellent advice. Another author said essentially the same thing when he said, "It ain't what a person don't know that hurts them, it's what they know that ain't so that hurts them." So true. Most of us buy into false concepts.

In last night's edition of the *Toronto Star*, a Gallup Poll of 1,003 adults was published on what those people believed was the cause of stress in their lives. More than 50 percent of people under fifty years of age believed that money and their jobs were the cause of their problems. Those people should definitely follow Holliwell's advice and examine their beliefs. They could eliminate much of their stress.

Jobs and money are never the primary cause of stress. Thinking, negative thinking, causes stress. The real cause of all problems lies in our thoughts, not in things or circumstances.

You and I possess the power to change our thoughts. It is our greatest power—the power to choose. If you are feeling stressed, choose to relax. Look at your problems as a stranger might. Then do something about them . . . NOW!

The best years of your life are the ones in which you
decide your problems are your own. You do not blame
them on your mother, the ecology, or the president.
You realize that you control your own destiny.

It is not in the stars to hold our destiny but in ourselves.

First comes thought; then organization of that thought,
into ideas and plans; then transformation of those
plans into reality. The beginning, as you will
observe, is in your imagination.

You Can Choose

How many times in a single day do you suppose you say, "I have to"? Count them. I'll bet you say or hear "I have to . . ." at least a hundred times between the time you get up in the morning and when you lie down at night.

I have to get the car fixed; I have to go shopping; I won't be home for dinner, I have to work. The truth is, you can go home for dinner if you really want to; you choose to work.

There is nothing you "have to" do. Everything you do, you choose to do.

I know you're probably thinking, "Now wait a minute, Proctor, there are some things a person has to do. You have to pay taxes." Think about it, my friend—you don't have to pay taxes. You have a choice of going to jail or moving to a tax-free zone.

I agree this may seem ridiculous, but it's true nevertheless.

J. Martin Kohe wrote a marvelous book titled *Your Greatest Power*. His book was about choice. The ability to choose is your greatest power. In fact, the ability to choose is what separates you from the rest of the animal kingdom.

Think of the number of times you are asked to go somewhere or to do something and you feel you have to. You don't. You have the ability to choose. You can say no! Are you aware that the word "no" can be a complete sentence? You may choose to be a little more diplomatic and suggest that you have chosen to do something else, rather than give a straight, flat NO—but it's your choice.

Give this some serious thought. Life is short, too short to be spent doing something or going somewhere you have not chosen to do or go. Many people stay in jobs they detest. Why? Another short, complete statement, "I quit," could change their lives.

It is your choice. Choose to have a great day! That is what I have chosen to do today.

Of the blessings set before you make
your choice, and be content.

The history of free men is never really written
by chance but by choice; their choice!

Our freedom can be measured by the number
of things we can walk away from.

CIRCUMSTANCES

Call Your Own Shots

Where we have been, where we are now, and where we are going. These are three important phases in everyone's life.

You can mentally mix exciting experiences from your past and present that will prepare you to develop an interesting vision for your future. Or, if you are not mentally alert, you could very easily reverse the process and reflect on some unpleasant experience or failure from your past that would cause you to see only the negative circumstances that exist in the present.

This sort of mental activity would automatically develop a negative attitude and prevent any productive planning for your future.

Our past experiences and our present circumstances have absolutely no power other than that which we choose to give them.

As each of us visits where we have been many times each day, get into the habit of giving your mental energy to your past accomplishments, your successes, the experiences that brought great joy into your life. You would then only see all of the opportunities that surround you. Positive circumstances will pop up one after another.

Where you are now suddenly becomes very exciting. Mentally mix that part with the present, and you will have difficulty containing yourself with the dynamic vision of your future.

Where you have been, where you are now, and where you are going. Three important phases. Make your mental mix a winning combination.

Many of the successful people I know keep a win list, a record of their accomplishments. They carry it with them and read it periodically.

You might try this. Then, when you look back, you will be certain of holding a beautiful picture.

- -

You are always free to change your mind and choose
a different future, or a different past.

Life is divided into three terms—that which was, which is,
and which will be. Let us learn from the past to profit by the
present, and from the present, to live better in the future.

- -

COMMUNICATION

Develop Your Intuition

There is a mental faculty we all possess that is often referred to as our "sixth sense"—intuition. Intuition is that sensitive mental tool that gives us the ability to pick up another person's moods, thoughts, vibrations, and feelings.

It's our "gut feel," so to speak.

Everyone has an intuitive factor and anyone can most certainly develop this mental faculty through exercise.

The very effective salespeople, police detectives, customs agents, etc., have a super-sensitive intuitive factor. That is the very reason they are so effective. They've trained themselves to pick up the other person's energy, as opposed to just hearing what the person is saying.

This has probably happened to you at least once in your lifetime. Think of the time people looked into your eyes and told you they loved you . . . and you knew they were lying. Or, when you sensed something was wrong with loved ones but they assured you everything was fine . . . only to find out later that they did, in fact, have a serious problem they were facing.

It was your intuitive factor that enabled you to pick up these unspoken messages.

To develop your intuitive factor and gain confidence in its use, you must have feedback. Whenever you are with people with whom you have built an excellent rapport, ask them for feedback. If you feel they are thinking about something, ask them. Your intuitive factor will actually pick up vibrations coming from that person.

Quite often, if you have a very close relationship with someone, you will pick up what that person is thinking, even before they verbally express it to you.

Vibrations never lie. A person could be saying one thing and, yet, thinking another. You will eventually get to the point where you will pay closer attention to the vibrations you are receiving than the words you are hearing.

Intuition is one of the most valuable mental tools you possess. Begin to consciously use it. Your rewards will be worth the effort.

Your time is limited, so don't waste it living someone
else's life. Don't be trapped by dogma—which is living
with the results of other people's thinking. Don't
let the noise of others' opinions drown out your
own inner voice. And most important, have the
courage to follow your heart and intuition.

—STEVE JOBS

The Great Compliment

If I had to choose the greatest asset for successful communication, I would have to say it is in our ability to listen.

Listening is a magnetic and strange thing, a creative force. The friends who listen to us are those we find ourselves moving toward, wanting to be with them, to be close to them.

When people are listened to, it stimulates them, enabling them to unfold and expand. Ideas actually begin to grow within them and come to life. It makes people happy and free when they are listened to. When we listen to people, an alternating current recharges us so that we never get tired of each other.

When people ask us to listen to them and we start giving advice, we have not done as they have asked. The moment we begin giving advice is the moment we begin trampling on their feelings.

When was the last time you sat down and genuinely listened—to your children, your spouse, or an associate in your business? Effective listening has been known to solve more ills than a truckload of pills.

Why not become a better listener today?

One point to remember—there is a difference between hearing and listening. You hear with your ears; you listen with your emotional mind. Give yourself to people without any thought or opinion of gain until you understand their position.

When you actively listen to other people, you are paying them a compliment. You actively listen with your eyes as well as your ears.

You listen with your intuitive factor. Even your body posture is an expression of active listening.

Yes, actively listening to someone is a sincere compliment. You are saying, I believe what you think matters.

. . . .

The wise man doesn't give the right answers,
he poses the right questions.

I like to listen. I have learned a great deal from listening
carefully. Most people never listen.

. . . .

COMPENSATION

More Than You're Being Paid For

Are you presently doing more than you are being paid for? Your answer to that question will probably be "Absolutely" or "Absolutely not."

There doesn't seem to be any halfway measure with this concept. There is a certain segment of the working population and, unfortunately, it is a large segment—that would probably suggest you seek psychiatric care if you answered "absolutely." However, if you check on where they are in life, you will find they are moving in the wrong direction and very likely picking up speed as they go.

In the vernacular, they are losing. To their way of thinking, it would be totally illogical to do more than they are being paid for. The law that governs their behavior is "Give me the money and then I will do the job."

However, the system that drives our economy does not work that way. It clearly states, "Do the job and then you get the money."

The worker or business that is always rewarded by the employer and customer alike is the one that delivers more than they were paid for.

The restaurant or vacation resort that gives you more than you paid for earns your repeat business. The salespeople who give extra service are the top salespeople. The employees who do not watch the clock, but put their heart and soul into their job and are never too busy to do more, are the ones who move ahead and are handsomely rewarded—if not by the company they work for, then by the companies that are waiting in the wings to get them.

Where do you stand? Review your behavior. Give a little more. You will be amazed and delighted with the rewards.

One might think that the money value of an invention
constitutes its reward to the man who loves his work. But . . .
I continue to find my greatest pleasure, and so my reward,
in the work that precedes what the world calls success.

CONFIDENCE

Divine Self-Confidence

A number of years ago, I wrote an article on self-confidence. I pointed out there are three types of self-confidence, but there is only one that will hold water.

The people who develop the proper type of self-confidence appear to live a charmed life. They are admired and respected by their peers.

A false self-confidence is nonproductive. This is when people have low self-esteem. However, their desire for acceptance and success causes them to put on a front. They tell themselves, I am not very good at what I do, but I want you to think I'm good at it.

The second type of confidence is a real form of confidence, but unfortunately never earns people the real joy that life offers. People with this type of confidence do what they do well, and they know it, but they make certain everyone else knows it as well.

This quickly turns into conceit.

The real winners have a divine self-confidence. They do what they do well, and they also know why. These fortunate individuals have an awareness of an infinite power that is within. They merely choose to build an image in their marvelous mind of what they want to do.

All of the truly great achievers in life have developed this divine self-confidence. It is the result of years of study and a self-imposed discipline. Happiness, health, and prosperity are their rewards.

If you have a divine self-confidence, you know how fortunate you are. If you don't, begin to study yourself. I can assure you, you will develop it.

Self-confidence is a must for a fulfilled life.

· ·

Faith is to believe what you do not see; the reward
of this faith is to see what you believe.

Our doubts are traitors and make us lose the good
we oft might win by fearing to attempt.

—WILLIAM SHAKESPEARE

· ·

The Safety Net Syndrome

Self-confidence is nothing more than knowledge. Let me say that again: To be self-confident, all you need is information.

Look at it this way. If you do something well, five thousand times, you know you can do it; therefore, you are confident.

If you have never done it before, you don't KNOW.

Without that knowledge, you doubt. If you want to be confident, then give yourself the chance to find out what your abilities are. By trying new things and taking the risk to stretch your present level of ability, you discover that trying is the key. You come to know that taking a chance is not the end of the world. You realize that security and peace are not the grounds on which self-confidence is developed.

Without at least trying, you know you are living well below your ability level.

Self-doubt is a progressive illness. When you refuse to risk and try confidence-building projects, you begin the downward spiral of rejecting growth opportunities and settling instead for the safety net of life.

That pattern is the safety net syndrome. You refuse to leave the nest; you don't try anything that, in any way, threatens the security and safety factors.

When was the last time you tried something you've never done before? When were you last exposed to some growth opportunity? By taking some risk and succeeding, you create that pattern of stretching your ability and increasing your knowledge about your skill level. What kind of a risk-taker are you?

Take some chances. You will develop more confidence. You have amazing potential. Stretch yourself! Be all that you can be!

- -

If you have no confidence in self, you are twice
defeated in the race of life. With confidence,
you have won even before you have started.

A great part of courage is the courage of
having done the thing before.

We gain strength, and courage, and confidence by each
experience in which we really stop to look fear in the face . . .
we must do that which we think we cannot.

- -

COURAGE

The Torchbearers

Theodore Roosevelt had six children from two marriages; two daughters and four sons. His youngest son, Quentin, was killed in an air battle over France in 1918 in World War I. He was only twenty-one years of age. This was just months prior to Roosevelt's own death in 1919.

Theodore Roosevelt wrote an epitaph for his son that is rich with truth and can serve as a form of inspiration for you and me.

Roosevelt said, "Only those are fit to live who do not fear to die, and none are fit to die that have shrunk from the joy of life. Both life and death are parts of the same great adventure. All of us who provide service and stand ready to sacrifice are the Torchbearers. We run with the torches until we fall, content if we can pass them to the hands of the other runner."

Theodore Roosevelt and his son Quentin were both, by his definition, Torchbearers.

How would you rate? Are you a Torchbearer?

If you want to live a full life, become one. They are the people who are always thinking of and helping others. Although Quentin Roosevelt died at twenty-one and his father, Theodore, at sixty-one, they both lived full, exciting, and dynamic lives. Study their records for yourself and you will be convinced.

Their lives have served as a great example for millions. Will your life do as much? If you are not a Torchbearer, become one today. The compensation is incredible.

. . . .

Inaction breeds doubt and fear. Action breeds confidence
and courage. If you want to conquer fear, do not sit
home and think about it. Go out and get busy.

You will never do anything in this world without courage.
It is the greatest quality of the mind next to honor.

You may have to fight a battle more than once to win it.

Courage is fear holding on a minute longer.

. . . .

Why Don't You?

In 1980 I moved to Atlanta from California. One Sunday morning I got up and decided to go to church. I wasn't particular about what church I attended, so I chose one from the phone book that I thought was nearby.

When I arrived at what I thought was the address, there was no church to be seen, just a big, beautiful white house sitting on about nine acres of magnificent land.

I noticed someone moving around, so I drove in and asked the person if they would please direct me to the church. The reply came with a smile from ear to ear. "Y'all here. This is the church!"

I was led into what I assumed had been the living room. The room had about fifty folding chairs and a small podium at one end. As I was quite early, the room was empty except for myself and the furniture.

Soon the room filled up, then a minister and a small but excellent choir filed in, making this old living room hot and crowded. However, the minister's talk was great. He really knew how to make you think. When I was leaving, Dr. Jay Dishman was at the front door. He made me feel more than welcome.

I returned the following week and was quite impressed. Jay not only remembered me, but he called me by name. When I was leaving I congratulated him on another fine sermon. Then I asked, "Why don't you build a church so it isn't as crowded and more people could hear you?"

He looked me square in the eye and replied, "Why don't you?"

Needless to say, I felt quite uncomfortable. I went home . . . but I later went back and accepted his challenge.

We raised more than a million dollars, and we built the church. Jay passed away recently and I flew to Atlanta to attend a service for him in his church. I lost a friend but was left with many memories. It was a nice feeling thinking we built a church.

Why are you waiting for someone else? Why don't you do it?

Let us not be content to wait and see what will happen, but give us the determination to make the right things happen.

Get action. Seize the moment. Man was never intended to become an oyster.

CREATIVITY

The Voice Within

Do you think of yourself as a creative personality?

If you do, you are both fortunate and correct.

Fortunate, because the majority of our population have been lulled into the false belief that some people are creative and others are not. Correct, because you are creative.

In fact, the beautiful truth is that everyone is creative. Although the behavior and conversation of many people would indicate that most people are not creative, the truth is not always in the appearance of things.

Study the idea of creativity. It will quickly become apparent that a small, select group have developed their creative potential while others have not.

If you are not developing your creative potential, I would urge you to begin.

We all desire more fullness in life, a greater and brighter vitality in ourselves, and less restriction in our surroundings. Our creative ability will enable us to enjoy this fullness and vitality in life.

It is wise to remember that the person who follows the crowd will get no farther than the crowd. The person who walks the creative path is likely to find they are in places no one has ever been before.

However, creativity in living is not without its attendant difficulties, for peculiarity breeds contempt. The unfortunate thing about being ahead of your time is that when people finally realize you were right, they will say it was obvious all along.

You have two choices in life. You can dissolve into the mainstream, or you can be distinct. To be distinct, you must be different. To be different, you must strive to be what no one else but you can be.

Don't be so concerned with the opinions of others; follow the quiet, creative voice from within.

. . . .

An essential aspect of creativity is not being afraid to fail.

Do not go where the path may lead, go instead
where there is no path and leave a trail.

. . . .

DECISION

Personal Power

*I once heard it said that the world will forgive you if
you make mistakes, but that life will not forgive you
if you fail to make decisions.*

With all the material that has been written on the subject of personal power, I seldom hear that decision making is the first principle in the development of your personal power.

The fear of making a decision is the result of fearing to make a mistake and, as Aldous Huxley once wrote, the fear of mistakes has a greater impact on you than making the mistakes.

Now would be a good time for you to get a notepad and write down three areas that affect you daily:

1. Where you are
2. Where you want to be
3. The steps needed to bridge the gap

This process will put you face-to-face with decisions you must make. As with every decision, there is the worst that could happen to you and the best that could happen to you. Write each side down and ask yourself what you would do if the worst happened, and then think of how much more beautiful life will be when the best happens.

This method by no means eliminates the risk you must take. But it does generate a more prepared mind and a more productive attitude for action. It also helps you become aware of some of the obstacles you must eliminate.

A study made of the lives of thousands of highly successful people showed that they all made decisions quickly and changed them very slowly, if and when they changed them at all.

Your personal power is moved into action by decision.

The materials of action are variable, but the use
we make of them should be constant.

—EPICTETUS

In any moment of decision, the best thing you can do is the
right thing, the next best thing is the wrong thing,
and the worst thing you can do is nothing.

Tough Decisions

The day before John F. Kennedy's inauguration, President Eisenhower told him that he would find no easy problems ever came to the President of the United States. He said if the problems were easy to solve, somebody else would have solved them.

Kennedy said he found that hard to believe, but came to realize it was true.

Abraham Lincoln had learned that lesson one hundred years earlier. Lincoln was no ordinary person. He had moved himself from a very ordinary station in life to a position where big decisions are made.

President Lincoln also learned that a position of responsibility not only brought with it big decisions, it also attracted numerous critics who would attack at every opportunity.

Those opportunities arose whenever he made a decision with which his critics did not agree.

It is recorded that a close friend of President Lincoln's once asked him if all of these attacks bothered him. Lincoln's answer was a classic, one you should keep in mind the next time you make a tough decision and you are openly criticized. He said: "If I were to try to read, much less answer, all the attacks made on me, this shop might as well be closed for any further business.

"I do the very best I know how—the very best I can; and I mean to keep doing so until the end. If the end brings me out all right, what is said against me won't amount to anything. If the end brings me out wrong, ten thousand angels swearing I was right would make no difference."

What a great attitude. It is also great advice to follow the next time you make a tough decision and are attacked by your critics.

Never bring the problem-solving stage into the decision-
making stage. Otherwise, you surrender yourself
to the problem rather than the solution.

In the final analysis there is no other solution to man's
progress but the day's honest work, the day's honest decision,
the day's generous utterances, and the day's good deed.

Management is doing things right; leadership
is doing the right things.

DIRECTION

The Two Most Important Ingredients

It has been believed, for too long a time and by too many people, that it takes above-average intelligence to succeed in business.

Although I don't imagine anyone considers intellectual competence a hazard, we should remember it is certainly no guarantee that success will accrue to all who possess it.

If intelligence is such an important ingredient in success, why do so many brilliant people fail? Why do so many fast starters lapse into mediocrity? While these two instances are not typical of brilliant people in general, they often do happen.

There are also many instances in which the level of success has little relationship to the level of intelligence. It has been observed, more frequently than chance would permit, that men and women of modest ability have reached the top of their organization or profession.

No one has ever been able to determine exactly what it takes to succeed in business, but there are certain characteristics that we know for certain contribute to success, regardless of a person's level of intelligence.

Successful people "learn from experience" and have "drive from within." They "believe in themselves." They have "power with people." They have "character."

Successful people have a sense of direction; they know where they are going and they know they will get there. They have developed an inner confidence that is expressed openly in their behavior and they have a genuine concern for the well-being of others.

Intelligence alone is not enough; it has never been enough on its own. You may be an ordinary student, but you can be an extraordinary success at whatever you choose to do when you enter the business world.

The two most important ingredients for a successful life are a goal and persistence.

If you're bored with life—you don't get up every
morning with a burning desire to do things—
you don't have enough goals.

Life can be pulled by goals just as surely as
it can be pushed by drives.

Persist and persevere, and you will find most
things that are attainable, possible.

DREAMS

Red Buick Convertible

I am forever talking about goals and the role they play in our lives. It's so important to understand the importance of a goal. It's not so much the goal that's important, it's the growth you experience en route to achieving your goal that's the big deal.

Without a goal it becomes easy—in fact, quite logical—to quit trying every time the going gets a little tough. It is the image in your mind of the goal reached that keeps you going regardless.

I came across an excellent story that illustrates this basic truth. It involved a young lady named Gertrude Ederle.

Up until the year 1926, no woman had ever swum the English Channel. Then an automobile company offered a red Buick convertible automobile and $2,000 in cash to the first woman who could accomplish this feat.

A nineteen-year-old American girl named Gertrude Ederle wanted the automobile. She could see herself with it. This image caused her to decide to swim the English Channel in order to get it.

Partway across the Channel, her body strength began to give

out and she felt she couldn't swim one more stroke. You may have some idea of how Gertrude must have felt.

But as she lay there waiting to be taken out of the water, she closed her eyes and before her imagination passed an image of herself sitting in this red Buick convertible. Seeing herself in possession of her goal gave her a new surge of strength, and she didn't stop again until she felt the sand of the opposite shore under her feet.

Swimming the Channel was not Gertrude Ederle's goal. The red Buick convertible was her goal. Swimming the Channel is what she had to do to reach her goal. The image of the goal gave her the necessary strength to keep going.

It worked for her, and it will work for you if you have a goal.

· ·

To accomplish great things, we must not only act,
but also dream; not only plan, but also believe.

What we need is more people who
specialize in the impossible.

· ·

EFFECTIVENESS

The Producers and the Almosts

The world has always cried for men and women who can get things done, for people who are self-starters, who see a task through to its finish.

It isn't how much you know but what you get done that the world rewards and remembers.

Millions of people are held back from success because they don't know how to get things done, more than any other single reason. It's the single biggest handicap to success—not lack of brains, not a lack of character or willingness.

These millions of people who fail to do something great with their lives know what to do and almost do it on time. They almost win promotions. They almost become leaders. They may miss by only a minute or by an inch, but they do miss, because they have never developed the ability to get things done.

The "Almosts" are not lazy. Often they are busier than the very effective few. They putter around all day long and half the night, though they fail to accomplish anything of any real importance. They are held back by indecision, by a lack of organization in their work, and by an overattention to minor details.

They are swirled around in circles, and they get nowhere because they don't chart a straight course and then stick to it.

You don't have to work harder; you must work more effectively. You must learn to make your work count. It is the Producers who raise the world's standard of living. It is the Producers who win the big share of the world's rewards. The Producers are those people who have developed the ability to get things done, and will not permit the Almosts to distract them.

. . . .

All men dream, but not equally. Those who dream
by night in the dusty recesses of their minds, wake in
the day to find that it was vanity: but the dreamers of
the day are dangerous men, for they may act on their
dreams with open eyes, to make them possible.

Seest thou a person diligent in their business?
They shall stand before kings.

—PROVERBS 22:29

. . . .

EFFORT

Worth It

Whatever you want to accomplish in this coming year has a price tag on it. You must give up something to get something. The greater the value, the greater the sacrifice required.

There is a high price to be paid for success, but you must realize that the rewards of true success are well worth the effort.

The highway to success is a toll road.

In Richard Bach's most provocative book, simply titled *One*, he raises many interesting questions in the reader's mind. He also gives beautiful, hopeful answers.

On the first page, the author makes a powerful statement: "I gave my life to become the person I am right now." Then he poses an interesting question:

"Was it worth it?"

Over the next twelve months, things in your life will change. You will find yourself in a different place, in a new condition, or your life may be much the same as it is today. Regardless, you will have paid another year of your life.

Amelia Barr hit the nail on the head when she said, "This world is run with far too tight a rein for luck to interfere. Fortune sells her wares; she never gives them. In some form or other, we pay for her favors."

Many people who are not pleased with their lot in life blame luck when they made the wrong choices, mixed with the wrong people, went down the wrong road. Orison Marden said, "What keeps so many people back is simply unwillingness to pay the price, to make the exertion, the effort to sacrifice their ease and comfort."

Make the coming year worthwhile. No one has a corner on success. It is yours for a price!

Great achievement is usually born of great sacrifice,
and is never the result of selfishness.

He who would accomplish little must sacrifice little;
he who would achieve much must sacrifice much;
he who would attain highly must sacrifice greatly.

Nothing ever comes to one, that is worth having,
except as a result of hard work.

—BOOKER T. WASHINGTON

ENTREPRENEURIALISM

Start Your Own Business

The other day I was talking with a young man who will graduate from university next month. He was having a very difficult time making a decision with respect to his future employment. What would he do? Where would he go?

On and on the questions flowed. However, the answers were escaping him.

I began by asking him how he wanted to live, and where he wanted to live.

Then I asked how much he wanted to earn. The amount he wanted to earn was considerably more than 99 percent of the companies in the country would offer, if they decided to employ him.

Then I asked, "Why don't you start your own company? Work for yourself." I suggested every company in the world was started by someone. If they could do it, he could, too.

His reply was a blank stare. Then slowly he said, "I never thought of that."

I replied, "There are millions of people in the country and every one of them has needs. Think of what those needs are, then which one you would most enjoy filling."

For some strange reason, as a people, we seem to think a person must be a certain age before they can start a business of their own. That idea has no foundation. It's ridiculous! Age has nothing to do with starting a business. Courage, ambition, and a sincere desire to serve others are all that are required. You may be eighteen or eighty.

I read where Kemmons Wilson built a chain of hotels—Wilson Inns. Mr. Wilson was eighty years old. He had retired and became bored. By the way, he is the originator of Holiday Inns.

Young Tim Dorchuk of Burlington, Ontario, at nineteen years of age, is a self-made millionaire. He started his own business at the age of twelve.

Experience . . . you will get it. Money . . . you will attract it. Make a decision, find a need, and fill it. Your age should not be a consideration.

Apathy can be overcome by enthusiasm, and enthusiasm can only be aroused by two things: first, an ideal, which takes the imagination by storm, and second, a definite intelligible plan for carrying that ideal into practice.

What would life be if we had no courage to attempt anything?

EXCELLENCE

Perfection

If you are in search of ideas that will stimulate you to greater results and rewards, permit me to suggest that you take a peek into history, or read biographies of great men and women from the past.

There is a wonderful biography written by John Addington Symonds on the life of one of the most famous Italians who has ever lived. The biography is titled *The Life of Michelangelo Buonarroti*.

Michelangelo Buonarroti was born over five hundred years ago. He was almost ninety years of age when he died, leaving the world with masterpieces that will live forever.

How does one do such work of perfection with lasting beauty?

Perhaps this question can be answered, in part, through a story about the time Michelangelo was putting some finishing touches to one of his statues when a friend came calling. A few days later his friend called again, and when he saw the statue he commented that the sculptor couldn't have done much to it since he was there last.

Michelangelo raised an eyebrow and replied, "I have retouched this part and polished that. I have softened this feature and brought out this muscle. I have given more expression to this lip and more energy to that limb."

"Oh yes," said his friend. "But all these are trifles."

"Perhaps so," replied Michelangelo. "But trifles make perfection—and perfection is no trifle." What a great lesson for us. Think of the times we skip over the trifles because we know no one will notice the difference. However, when the trifles are all molded together, they spell "perfection."

Although you may never reach perfection, taking care of the trifles will definitely improve the quality of your work, and you will be rewarded accordingly.

It is reasonable to have perfection in our eye that
we may always advance toward it, though
we know it can never be reached.

Shoot for the moon. Even if you miss,
you'll land among the stars.

EXPERIENCE

Take That Trip

All successful people are forever attempting to expand their horizons; to stretch their minds. Oliver Wendell Holmes put it beautifully when he said, "Once the mind has been expanded by a big idea, it will never go back to its original state."

Holmes was right. When you have expanded your mind, you have developed a greater awareness, and awareness is not something you can lose.

Traveling can do this for you.

I have been fortunate enough to have traveled completely around this shrinking globe you and I live on. I was running around Brazil when I was eighteen. I have strolled through the streets of Suva in Fiji, had dinner at a home in Takapuna, New Zealand, played golf in Barbados, lived in Sunbury-on-Thames in England, and been entertained at the Lido in Paris.

All of these places and countless others I can return to at will, in my memories. They are fond memories. Every one of these experiences in other places has broadened my mind. I recently spoke with a cabdriver in Barbados who was in his forties and had never been off the island. Although I love Barbados—it's my most favorite spot to rest and relax—I couldn't help but feel sorry for him, because he had nothing in his personal experience to compare it to. Where would you like to go and take your loved one? Why don't you make a firm decision this very minute to go? Set a date, book your flight. Don't even think about what the trip will cost. If you plan to go one year from today and amortize the cost over a year, it will be very little each day.

Make a game out of it. Each day put away the necessary amount. When the time comes to leave, your trip will be paid for. You will also find that one of the most enjoyable parts of your trip will be looking forward to going. Traveling. It will make you a more interesting person.

. . . .

We shall not cease from exploration, and the end
of all our exploring will be to arrive where we started
and know the place for the first time.

—T. S. ELIOT

The traveler sees what he sees, the tourist
sees what he has come to see.

How often I found where I should be going only
by setting out for somewhere else.

. . . .

FAITH AND BELIEF

Bigger Than the Evidence

Someone once defined faith as believing in spite of the evidence that indicates failure.

A friend of mine recently had his business all but wiped out by a theft, which cleaned out his inventory. Through some oversight, his insurance did not cover the stock, leaving him with an empty warehouse.

The local newspapers carried a lengthy article detailing my friend's dilemma, stating that he was virtually out of business. You must admit, the evidence of being totally wiped out is rather overwhelming.

But not in my friend's mind.

His attitude is, "This is the way I started, and I will start the very same way again." This condition would drive many away, but his faith is much stronger than the evidence.

What about you? Is there evidence in your life holding you back from going ahead, from starting again? It would be impossible to estimate the number of people who are held back because they allow the evidence to overwhelm them. On the other hand, you could easily recount the number of people who were once faced with impossible odds and succeeded because of one single piece of evidence in their favor: FAITH. They would have done it, no matter how great the odds were against them.

The people in that category felt it would be better to try and not succeed, than to not have tried at all. This explosive power of faith in oneself has a domino effect. It knocks over any number of obstacles and picks up momentum as it moves forward.

My friend and his partner proved, once again, that all of us are bigger than the evidence that indicates failure.

You can prove this to yourself when you decide to move forward toward one obstacle at a time, and with a strong faith, you will increase the possibility of winning.

A man of courage is also full of faith.

We can let circumstances rule us, or we can take charge and rule our lives from within.

The Deciding Factor

There are countless stories of men and women who had great purpose and high ideals, and who worked toward and reached incredible goals.

Time after time, these people came up against obstacles or circumstances that would destroy the average person.

These people would find themselves in situations that appeared devastating. They might have lost fortunes or loved ones, or possibly had to battle some great physical problem, but they never appeared to waver.

It seemed as if nothing could stop them.

You very likely can think of a number of people you know personally, or know of, who are giants when it comes to producing in your industry. The history of sports is filled with such examples as well.

What made these people great was their belief, or faith. It was unshakable. No one and nothing could disturb or destroy their faith.

It could very easily appear as if some emotional or capricious God has singled out, reached out to, and touched these individuals and caused them to do such great things.

But everyone, including YOU, has been touched, blessed, endowed with these tools. You must develop a belief or faith based on understanding, just as these people did for themselves. Their faith was not blind, the kind that is easily shattered like fine crystals with the first knock that comes along. Their faith had a strong foundation based on understanding.

These people are often referred to as spiritual people, and it is not difficult for them to believe or have faith, because they KNOW. They know they can do whatever they visualize. They know they are dynamic, creative beings.

And so are you.

Faith is a knowledge within the heart,
beyond the reach of proof.

Man is made by his belief. As he believes, so he is.

Faith indeed tells what the senses do not tell,
but not the contrary of what they see.
It is above them and not contrary to them.

Positive Beliefs

When you believe something, it stays with you wherever you go; you cherish your beliefs and often go to great lengths to defend them whenever they are challenged.

What do you believe about yourself?

If you're like most people, you probably believe you are ten pounds overweight, or maybe that you should have stayed in school, or should have paid more attention to your parents' advice . . . the list of beliefs goes on and on.

The vast majority of our population believes fairly negative concepts about themselves. They know or understand very little about themselves; how beautiful and powerful they truly are.

You should have good and sound reasons for all of your beliefs. Most, if not all, of these false beliefs we hold were picked up when we were children and have never been questioned. They are then used as excuses to justify poor performance. Negative beliefs are a useless, nonproductive waste of mental and physical energy.

Around the turn of the nineteenth century, William James said, "Believe and your belief will create the fact."

If you hold negative beliefs about yourself, you can be sure that your results will prove you right. However, clearly understand that the opposite is also true. When you hold powerful, positive beliefs about yourself, your results will reflect how accurate your beliefs are.

If you are not happy with the way your life is going, question your beliefs. Get a good book or audio program and learn many of the beautiful truths about yourself. You will find that studying the positive aspects of yourself will be an exciting adventure, and you will be openly rewarded for the time and effort you put into this project.

No man has the right to dictate what other men should perceive, create or produce, but all should be encouraged to reveal themselves, their perceptions and emotions, and to build confidence in the creative spirit.

As is our confidence, so is our capacity.

Let's not be narrow, nasty, and negative.

FEAR

Seek the Unknown

Some time ago I was reading an article by the late Earl Nightingale. He explained that it is an ageless human trait to fear the unknown—to assume that what has never been tried or seen must be bad, horrible, or dangerous; and it's this same ancient human trait that keeps many of us from exploring new possibilities.

Back in early history there were mapmakers who, with the instruments and knowledge of their time, did their best to map the known world.

Some did surprisingly well, but they all had one interesting trait in common. When they came to the limits of their knowledge—and their world was smaller in those days—they would write on their maps, "Beyond this point is great danger." On some they would write, "Beyond this point are dangerous creatures." And the sad part is, people believed it and would not step beyond what was mapped.

In your career, with your goals, in your relationships, have you drawn a map of the area you will not step beyond because of what is unknown, because there is a chance you might fail?

If so, why not consider the possibility of what good is beyond your present comfort zone, and that the only requirement to travel this path is the ability to act; the ability to make the necessary attempts to move you from where you are to where you want to be.

How often do we find ourselves taking the known way rather than the unknown, only because it is more comforting and less challenging—but never more rewarding?

When you begin to map out your journey to success, there will be many areas you may not want to enter because you are unfamiliar with them. However, once you do enter, you are exposed to the greatest reward life has to offer: awareness.

. . . .

Our doubts are traitors and make us lose the good
we oft might win by fearing to attempt.

—WILLIAM SHAKESPEARE

Don't let the fear of striking out hold you back.

Make voyages. Attempt them. There's nothing else.

—TENNESSEE WILLIAMS

. . . .

The Terror Barrier

The first ten years of my stay here on planet Earth were spent in Owen Sound, Ontario. I can vividly remember the hot summer day I was taken by an older member of my family to Harrison Park, where there was a fine swimming pool. The older kids were going up the ladder and jumping or diving off the high diving board. They were having a great time. Wanting to be accepted by the older kids, I, too, went up the ladder—reluctantly, but I climbed it.

I will never forget the terror that gripped my mind and body when I looked down. Their coaxing did absolutely no good. There was no way I was going off that board. I climbed back down the ladder.

That was the first time in my life that I can recall coming up against the Terror Barrier. I not only lost out on the excitement and thrill that would have been gained by jumping. I also lost a little self-respect.

If you think hard enough, you will recall the first time you came face-to-face with the Terror Barrier. You either stepped through it to freedom or back into bondage, imprisoned by your own fears.

I continued to step back from anything I truly feared until I was twenty-six years of age. Then with the encouragement of a caring person, I said, "No more." And I have been free ever since.

The Terror Barrier comes up in front of us every time we attempt to make a major move in life, into an area we have never traveled before.

I have sold businesses in Canada, the United States, and England for years, and I could not even guess at the number of times I have sat with men and women who have come right up to that barrier, wanting to go ahead, but were not able to. These were people who could have succeeded and wanted to, but didn't.

Is that Terror Barrier holding you or your business back? Do what I did and crash through. You won't regret it.

Glory lies in the attempt to reach one's
goal and not in reaching it.

Attempt the impossible in order to improve your work.

FOCUS

Chatter of the Masses

Reader's Digest is a great publication. It always has a number of articles that are mentally stimulating. The following unattributed lines were picked up from a Reader's Digest a number of years ago:

"Small minds talk about people. Average minds talk about events. Great minds talk about ideas."

I have come to believe this is fairly accurate.

I suppose we all fall into the first two categories—talking about people and events—periodically.

However, have you ever noticed that those two categories dominate the conversation of most people? Listen carefully and you will hear a buzz of meaningless noise going on around you almost constantly.

It would almost appear as if people were under some obligation to talk, whether they had anything to say or not.

I refer to this as the "chatter of the masses." If you are not mentally on guard, you will be swept into this useless waste of time and energy. If you don't consciously and deliberately create order in your mind, your environment or the people surrounding you will dictate your mental state of being.

Observe those who are surrounding you on any given occasion. Their conversation and actions could very easily change completely four or five times in less than a minute.

If you think I am exaggerating, check this out for yourself or possibly get involved with a few people in conversation and deliberately change the topic as often as possible—four or five times a minute. If you don't tell them what you're doing, they will never notice, but they will willingly follow.

What does this mean? Well, your mind is the greatest power in the universe. If you're not diligent, you will waste it and go nowhere.

Consciously choose to associate with those great souls who discuss BIG ideas.

Small things amuse small minds.

Like associates with like.

That Force Unseen

James Allen, the wonderful Victorian author, wrote about the human will in his masterpiece, As a Man Thinketh: *"The human Will, that force unseen, / The offspring of a deathless Soul / Can hew a way to any goal / Though walls of granite intervene."*

James Allen was correct. Your will is the mental faculty that gives genuine power to your ideas. The biographies and autobiographies of great men and women all indicate they had the ability to stay focused on their chosen objectives.

If you have a sincere desire to become mentally strong, you must exercise your will. It is absolutely essential that you develop your ability to concentrate.

The most effective executives and all of the great salespeople have this outstanding ability. They are not easily distracted. Try and imagine a heart surgeon who has not developed the ability to give undivided attention to what he or she is doing.

I am certain you would not want to be their patient.

Try this exercise every day for thirty days. Sit in your favorite chair and hold a candle in your hands. Light the candle and stare at the flame. If your attention begins wandering, immediately bring it back to the flame of the candle.

If in the beginning you have difficulty keeping your mind focused, don't worry about it. Continue with this exercise four or five minutes at a time, two or three times a day. Within a month, your ability to focus will become automatic.

This simple exercise can assist you in developing a very powerful will.

Remember: Concentration, intense concentration, gives real power to your ideas. When you begin to master your ability to concentrate on one thing, you can concentrate on virtually anything . . . and that's an invaluable skill to possess.

. . . .

Concentration is my motto—first honesty,
then industry, then concentration.

Concentrate all your thoughts upon the work at hand.
The sun's rays do not burn until brought to a focus.

. . . .

FREEDOM

Set Yourself Free

Do you think of Shakespeare as being a highbrow author who wrote plays designed to bore high school students? Do you view his writings as something for other people—writings that have nothing to do with the practical problems of life?

If your answer is yes, think again. Shakespeare was not a way-out, but a way-in kind of guy.

I quote, "Every bondman in his own hand bears the power to cancel his captivity." How can you apply Shakespeare's advice in a practical manner to today?

"Every bondman"—what does he mean? Every person who feels they are in bondage in any way . . . who feels trapped by circumstances . . . who seems bound to failure, poverty, sickness . . . who seems held back from what would make their life complete and good.

"Every bondman in his own hand bears"—that is, he possesses

within himself the power to cancel or get rid of his captivity, his seeming bondage.

You can be free. You have the power within you to remove the shackles that bind you.

Paul Carus wrote in *The Gospel of Buddha*, "People are in bondage, because they have not removed the idea of 'I.'" Leland Val Van de Wall wrote, "Let us not look back in anger, nor forward in fear, but around us in awareness."

The only power our problems can have over us is the power we give to them. As Emerson wrote, "The only thing that can grow is the thing we give energy to."

If you are in bondage, held captive by problems, you have the power in your own hands to set yourself free. You are the only one who can set you free.

Shakespeare said it, I believe it, and that settles it . . . for me.

. . . .

Freedom lies in being bold.

Money won't create success, the freedom to make it will.

It does not take a majority to prevail . . . but rather
an irate, tireless minority, keen on setting brushfires
of freedom in the minds of men.

. . . .

GOALS

The Essence of Life

Do you sometimes find life a little dull or perhaps boring? Life can be an exciting adventure, but you must make the excitement . . . discover the adventure.

Chris Rasmussen and her husband, Stan, are friends of mine. Chris sent me an article about the late John Goddard, which was in the *Deseret News*.

I doubt if Goddard had a dull or boring moment in his life. When he was fifteen he listed 127 challenging goals, which he tenaciously pursued. Among his challenges, he listed exploring the Nile, the world's largest river, and the Congo, the second-largest; climbing Mount Everest as well as the Matterhorn in a raging blizzard; running a five-minute mile; and playing "Claire de Lune" on the piano—all of which he fulfilled.

At the time of my writing this broadcast, John Goddard had accomplished 108 of the original challenges. A new goal, not on the list he set originally, was flying the sleek, supersonic B-1 bomber, the U.S. Air Force's most advanced plane. It can fly at supersonic speeds unnoticed under a radar blanket. He made the flight on November

3, 1989, in Abilene, Texas, after gaining approval from the secretary of the air force. Goddard had already flown forty-seven different types of aircraft, including the F-4 Phantom, F-11 fighter-bombers, and the F-106 Delta Dart.

John Goddard climbed twelve of the world's highest mountains, conducted fourteen major expeditions into remote regions, traversed fifteen of the world's most treacherous rivers, visited 120 countries, and studied 260 primitive tribes.

Goal setting is the essence of life. Do these things not for external praise but for inner reward. It makes you a better person, parent, and professional. It is important to be constantly growing.

Human beings must have action; and they
will make it if they cannot find it.

He who attends to his greater self becomes a great man, and
he who attends to his smaller self becomes a small man.

Periods of tranquility are seldom prolific of creative
achievement. Mankind has to be stirred up.

The Goal Card

Over the past twenty to twenty-five years I have given away a few hundred thousand goal cards. Whenever I speak at a convention or a seminar I always have one put on every seat. We freely give them to companies or managers in corporations, to hand out to employees.

The reaction of the individuals receiving the cards is always interesting. Frequently, a person will pick one up, look at it, smile, and lay it down again. It would appear as if the person is thinking, "Isn't that cute." Others will quickly snap it up and ask for more.

It is merely a card in a plastic sleeve with a positive statement on one side and a place for the person to write their goal on the other side. We recommend the person carry the card loose in their purse or pocket. Then, every time they touch the card, they begin thinking of their goal.

Try it. Whatever you write on the card, you will ultimately get . . . IF you continue to carry and read the goal card.

Research indicates that only 13 percent of us have clearly defined goals. A clear 87 percent of us have no clearly defined direction in life. Only 3 percent of us have our goal in writing. But the 3 percent that do enjoy the highest incomes. They lead meaningful, exciting lives.

I began carrying a card in my pocket with my goal written on it back in 1961. I found that it works like unadulterated magic. The idea of the goal card may be cute, but it is also extremely effective.

What do you seriously want? Do you know? If you do, try writing it on a card and carrying it with you. The results will amaze and delight you.

. . . .

If one advances confidently in the direction of his dreams,
and endeavors to live the life which he has imagined, he will
meet with a success unexpected in common hours.

—HENRY DAVID THOREAU

Practice yourself, for heaven's sake in little things,
and then proceed to greater.

. . . .

Start Right Now

A few years ago, a young but excellent salesperson gave me a recording of a speech a minister out of Minneapolis had delivered to a sales convention in the United States. He said something in his speech I don't suppose I shall ever forget.

The minister said that the saddest thing when he is officiating at a funeral is not the death of the body but the death of all the dreams.

Did he ever hit the nail on the head with that line. Think of the millions that go to their graves with the music still in them.

They never had any goals.

It was the house they were going to build and never built; or the business they were going to start; the car they longed to own; the trip they were going to take.

What do you want to be, do, or have? Make up your mind this very instant that you will accomplish it. Absolutely refuse to wait another day to begin working toward your goal.

James Allen, in his wonderful little book *As a Man Thinketh*, said, "Your circumstances may be uncongenial, but they shall not long remain so if you but perceive an Ideal and strive to reach it."

Forget about waiting until all your circumstances are favorable. Start right now. Begin by making a clearly defined written statement of your goal. Write your goal on a card and carry it with you and read it many times every day. This might sound like immature behavior, but believe me, it works for everyone who will do it.

This one act is what separates the poor from the rich, the weak from the strong, the sad from the happy.

The most fulfilled human being is the one who is always pursuing meaningful goals.

People with goals succeed because they know where they're going. It's as simple as that.

Our goals can only be reached through a vehicle of a plan, in which we must fervently believe, and upon which we must vigorously act. There is no other route to success.

GRATITUDE

My Eleven Loveliest Things

It is unfortunate but true that for many people, "life" is something that is going to happen in the future. They are always looking forward to the arrival of that big event or that big day.

While I am certainly a strong proponent of goals or objectives, I firmly believe we should attempt to be consciously aware of the many wonderful little events we are involved with in the present. Life is now. It can and should be enjoyed.

I recently came across something written by a little Scottish girl titled "My 11 Loveliest Things—People Not Counted." This little girl understood how to enjoy the little things that happen every day. Permit me to share her list with you.

1. The scrunch of dry leaves as you walk through them
2. The feel of clean clothes
3. Water running into the bath
4. The cold of ice cream
5. Cool wind on a hot day

6. Climbing up and looking back
7. Honey in your mouth
8. Smell of a pie baking
9. Hot water bottle in bed
10. Babies smiling
11. Baby kittens

I don't know about you, but I'm sure I would like that little Scottish girl. Number nine, the hot water bottle in bed, tells some of us her list was made some time ago, since many people today would have no idea why anyone would put a hot water bottle in a bed.

Her list is a good idea. Take the time today to make such a list. Your eleven loveliest things—people not counted. You will find that making such a list will quiet your mind, relieve tension, and probably help you focus on what you are presently doing that is enjoyable.

It is called living.

Enjoy your day!

Gratitude bestows reverence, allowing us to encounter everyday epiphanies, those transcendent moments of awe that change forever how we experience life and the world.

Gratitude is the sign of noble souls.

Gratitude is the fairest blossom which springs from the soul.

GROWTH

No One Ever Arrives

I want to suggest that you think of where you are in life; the success you are enjoying. Think of what it took to get you where you are.

Whatever it took to get you to the point you're at will not be sufficient to keep you there. No one ever arrives. You're either improving your position, or you are sliding backward.

How often have we watched successful people fall from grace after reaching the pinnacle of their selected career?

We need to keep pursuing, keep on doing and looking for new and better ways to grow and expand beyond the position we have reached.

Have you ever heard the statement that all people want to grow, but not everyone wants to make the necessary changes to grow? These individuals fail to recognize the most permanent of all laws; that is, change.

Many major corporations, some of which were considered institutions, have literally disappeared because of their mistaken belief that they had arrived.

I am not speaking here of change for change's sake, but rather, change for the sake of growth. It matters not how much we change, provided we are changing, improving, growing.

To continue positive motion in our personal, family, and business lives, we need a track to run on. We need to ask ourselves deep, penetrating questions as a constant checkup.

The answers will always come when we have a constant stream of provoking questions. Be prepared and willing to make whatever productive changes are required.

Without continual growth and progress, such words
as "improvement," "achievement," and
"success" have no meaning.

Life is growth. If we stop growing, technically
and spiritually, we are as good as dead.

HABIT

The Common Things

George Washington Carver lived an interesting life. If you are inclined to learn from the real giants of history, Carver's life is one you could learn a lot from.

He once said, "When you can do the common things of life in an uncommon way, you will command the attention of the world."

Forming the habit of doing the common things in life in an uncommon way will not only command the attention of the world. It will also guarantee you an interesting life—a life that is filled with satisfaction every day.

You and I invest a respectable part of every day involved in doing common things. Frequently, because these common things do not seem important, they get done with very little thought.

Isolated or standing by themselves, the common things probably are not very important. However, when you line the common things up, put them back to back, they become very important. Doing them in an uncommon way is what separates the amateur from the pro.

The author Dr. Robert A. Russell said that developing greatness in one's life is simple; anyone can do it. You merely do little things in a great way every day. Russell and Carver were essentially giving us the same advice.

It worked for them, and it will work for you.

Do what they suggested today. Commit to perform every task you tackle today in an uncommon way, regardless of how common it might be. Go the extra mile . . . put your heart and soul into your work and refuse to permit the goof-offs to distract you. When you lie down tonight you will reflect with pride and satisfaction on your day. Then, do the same tomorrow.

In fact, why not make a habit of it!

- -

There are no menial jobs, only menial attitudes.

Repetition of the same thought or physical action develops into a habit which, repeated frequently enough, becomes an automatic reflex.

A superior man is modest in his speech, but exceeds in his actions.

- -

HAPPINESS

Zest for Life

Sometimes we lose sight of the value of our work, and consequently we lose the zest for life—not just from our work, but from our lives.

Here are a few zest-restoring ideas that you can use RIGHT NOW and every day from now on.

1. Understand that anything, your job, marriage, etc., regardless of how exciting in the beginning, will grow—not *may* grow—*will* grow stale in time, if you are not careful.
2. Keep in mind that we must fight staleness in our lives daily. There is something that you can do—something that you must do—every day in order to keep vitality in your performance. It's simply the actor's technique. Live the part or act the part.
3. Realize that there is no such thing as a job without a future. Every job has a future, just as every person has. Whether that future is great or small will depend

entirely upon the person. There are no small parts, there are only small actors.

4. See the big picture (with you in it). See your job in relation to the whole scheme of things. Remember, only you place the limitation on you, regardless of what THEY might say.

5. Finally, continue to develop your ability to see yourself, your work, and what you do through the eyes of the most important person—The Customer.

In times of unrest and in an unstable economy, it is very easy to let your attitude slip and begin feeling sorry for yourself. This is precisely when you want to practice healthy attitudinal rules to stay alert, alive, and enthusiastic.

Don't ever lose the zest for life, and life won't lose its zest for you. Say something positive to every person you meet today.

Nothing great in the world has ever been accomplished without passion.

Pleasure in the job puts perfection in the work.

IDEAS

Double Your Business

For some strange reason, most individuals mentally fool around with a small idea when they begin to think of increasing their business. It is 5 to 10 or 15 percent, if they even give consideration to an increase.

I want to suggest that you begin to think of doubling your business. That's right. Doubling it.

If you are the chairman of Exxon or some other multinational corporation, the idea is probably ridiculous. However, odds are, you are not in that position. Even if you are, you can double your effectiveness.

Think with me for a moment. It takes no more energy to work on a big idea than it does to work on a small one, so you can proceed assured that this type of mental activity will not give you a brain hernia.

Take a sheet of paper and put a figure at the top that will represent twice the business you are presently doing. If you are in a position where your effectiveness is not measured in dollars, write down what you would be doing when you are twice as effective.

Then write the words "How can I?" When you begin to think about this, ideas will probably begin flying into your mind explaining why you can't. They will, in all probability, be valid but counterproductive. Forget them. Tell yourself you have nowhere to write them. Keep thinking. After a while, positive ideas will begin to flow.

Write all of them on your paper, even the ridiculous ones.

These positive ideas will prime your pump for better ideas. Al Spizzirri, a friend of mine in Toronto, took his income from $18,000 a year to $500,000 in two short years with this concept.

Our seminar company expanded across Canada into all of the United States, Australia, and New Zealand by using it.

Double your business—it's an exciting idea.

Vision is the art of seeing what is invisible to others.

IMAGINATION

Goal Achievers

Take the lid off your marvelous mind and dream. Goal Achievers do not limit themselves. There is no reason why you cannot have the good you desire, if you can see yourself with it. Your imagination is one of your most marvelous mental faculties.

Do what all Goal Achievers do and use it properly.

There are people who always play it safe. They never tackle more than they are sure they can handle without effort and risk. Thus they invite neither triumph nor defeat. They never learn the greatness of their mental ability or the strength of their endurance.

On the contrary, Goal Achievers are potential pathfinders, eagerly in search of a trail to blaze. Make sure your goal is big and interesting enough to really fire up your emotions.

Only you can decide what your goal is going to be. Although another person—your spouse, parent, employer, or associate—may offer suggestions, you and only you can make the final decision.

There are no other people in the entire world who are capable of setting your goal for you. If they try, and they probably will, do not permit it to happen. You will not commit yourself to other people's goals or one you set to please others.

Your goal should be something you want, not something you need. There is no inspiration in needs; there is only inspiration in wants. The goal does not have to be logical; in fact, you will probably be much more inspired if it is totally illogical.

The road to your goal may be a rough one; therefore, it is very important for you to be very emotionally involved with the idea of reaching your goal.

. . . .

Imagination grows by exercise, and contrary to common belief, is more powerful in the mature than in the young.

High achievement always takes place in the framework of high expectation.

The desire for safety stands against every great and noble enterprise.

. . . .

The "How" Will Come

Unsuccessful people know that lack of action is safe and very rarely causes them to stretch. Imagine for a moment a person refusing to drive to work until all the traffic lights were green.

Seems ridiculous, doesn't it?

Yet that is precisely the way many people live their lives. They refuse to mentally entertain ideas for any length of time because they are uncertain as to how they can carry out or accomplish those ideas.

Never reject a goal simply because you don't have the whole picture. Never reject a fantastic dream because you presently do not have all of the resources, manpower, or expertise to bring that goal into reality. Hold on to magnificent goals even if they seem impossible to attain at the time.

Airplanes would not exist today if the Wright brothers had forgone their incredible idea because they didn't know at the start how the idea would work, where they would get the money to finance the project, or where to find the people needed to see their goal manifest itself into physical form.

Set clear objectives for your life and don't worry about how the goal will come to fruition. Set the goal and lock into it. Just see the end result.

If you can create the picture, and lock into it, the method of how it will be accomplished will come. Remember, too, not to concern yourself at this time with whether you're comfortable with the idea or not. That isn't important at this point. The belief and the method of accomplishing it will come, provided you persist.

Carlyle said, "Go as far as you can see. When you get there, you will see how you can go further."

. . . .

No great deed is done by falterers who ask for certainty.

Dream lofty dreams, and as you dream, so you shall become.
Your vision is the promise of what you shall one day be; your
ideal is the prophecy of what you shall at last unveil.

. . . .

INDIVIDUALISM

You Are Different

Henry Ford was once quoted as saying, "All Fords are exactly alike, but no two men are just alike. Every new life is a new thing under the sun; there has never been anything just like it before, never will be again. A young man ought to get that idea about himself; he should look for the single spark of individuality that makes him different from other folks, and develop that for all he is worth. Society and schools may try to iron it out of him; their tendency is to put it all in the same mold, but I say don't let that spark be lost; it is your only real claim to importance."

That was excellent advice Ford left us, and it is worthy of considerable and serious thought.

Countless millions of people spend their lives trying to be what others want them to be and doing what other people expect them to do. They force themselves into patterns of behavior that have been established for, and by, people with personalities entirely different from their own.

Seeking to conform to those patterns, they dissolve into blurred mirror images as they snuff out their spark of individuality to imitate others. Rootless and dissatisfied, they strive frantically, and most often vainly, to find their own identities within the constricting limits of an existence alien to their own natures, instincts, and innate desires.

Why?

It takes courage to step out on your own and do your own thing . . . regardless of what others around you are doing. We have a tendency to follow the crowd, probably because that is what we were taught to do. In school, we were encouraged to be just like all the other good little boys and girls. Was that a bad thing? For some yes, for others no. Some people just never broke out of that habit and never developed their own individuality.

We all admire the courageous person and quite often consider the individual who lacks courage a coward. However, that is not how Earl Nightingale saw it. He said that the opposite of courage was not cowardice; it was conformity.

I believe the more you think about that, the more you will be inclined to agree with him. It does take courage to break away from the crowd, to go against the norm. It takes courage to stand up for the person who is being unjustly criticized rather than agreeing and going along with the crowd. It takes courage for the teenager to say no when all the rest of the kids begin going down the wrong path.

Have you taken the time to think of what makes you different? If you haven't, you should. Take my advice and do as Henry Ford said: "Develop that difference for all you are worth."

The next time you are encouraged to fall in line, to be a sport, and everything in you says no, be courageous and go your own way. There is no compensation in conformity.

. . . .

The secret to happiness is freedom . . . And the
secret to freedom is courage.

. . . .

INNOVATION

Un-Common Sense

You must be careful of those much-abused terms "common sense" and "conscience." Both are based on moral standards of the times and the accepted opinions of the masses. "Un-common sense" is truly the priceless ingredient that stands behind all progress and inventions.

It was not long ago that the world was considered flat because it was "common sense" to believe so.

Samuel Morse could not get the consent of the state of New Jersey to have poles erected so he could send messages from New York to Pennsylvania. Morse was refused on the grounds that it was not "common sense" to send a message through a wire by tapping on an instrument.

When the Wright brothers first began to fly at Kitty Hawk, North Carolina, it took a long time before the masses would believe they were actually doing it. It wasn't "common sense."

Do a little research and you will find that at the turn of the nineteenth century it was not proper for a female to lie on a beach in a bathing suit that did not completely hide her anatomy. Those who dared to break the rigid rules of society and its conceptions of decency were severely criticized and punished. Society saw to it that they suffered from pangs of "conscience."

Today, of course, people can enjoy the sunshine and the beaches without inhibition—the "common sense" of today is much healthier than the "common sense" of yesterday.

Our present way of life is based on moral standards that were branded years ago as "indecent" or "impossible"—and yet we are improving all the time.

Identify yourself with growth and progress by using your God-given faculties more fully. Use "un-common sense."

. . . .

I cannot help fearing that men may reach a point where
they look on every new theory as a danger, every
innovation as a toilsome trouble, every social advance
as a first step toward revolution, and that they
may absolutely refuse to move at all.

The advancement and diffusion of knowledge
is the only guardian of true liberty.

Think different.

. . . .

THE LAW OF ATTRACTION

Good Vibrations

Have you ever spent time wondering why some people continually attract negative situations into their lives, while others seem to attract nothing but beautiful situations into theirs?

The concept behind this "law of attraction" contains power, possibility, and promise if you will use it.

You are a living, breathing, creative magnet. You have the ability to control what you attract into your life. Why not make a conscious decision to attract into your life all of the good you desire? Historically, there have always been small, select groups of individuals who were aware of how to work in harmony with this natural law of the universe . . . the law of attraction.

This law clearly states that you can only attract to you that which is in harmony with you. Everything in this universe vibrates, including your mind and body. Look at your body through a microscope. It is a mass of energy—moving, vibrating.

Your mind controls the vibration you are in at any given moment. You control your mind by the thoughts you choose. No one can cause you to think something you don't want to think. This is where freedom comes in.

This is also where the problem begins with most people. They permit what is happening around them to determine how they think.

Ninety percent of the population wish positive but think negative. Their negative thoughts put them in a negative vibration, which, by law, determines what is attracted into their lives.

As a creative individual, you will continually attract good things into your life by thinking positive thoughts and expecting the best life has to offer. You deserve it.

Science is a way of thinking much more
than it is a body of knowledge.

Man, alone, has the power to transform his thoughts
into physical reality; man, alone, can dream
and make his dreams come true.

—NAPOLEON HILL

LEADERSHIP

Which Will You Be?

People are not leaders by virtue of their position. No, real leadership involves much more. You might be the boss, might have President or General Manager on your business card, but that does not make you a leader.

Leadership involves the ability to lead. A leader is someone who knows where he/she is going and is able to persuade others to go along.

An organization short on money can borrow and one with poor facilities can build, but if it's short on leadership, the likelihood of it surviving for any length of time is very poor.

What makes an exceptional leader? Here are a few of their characteristics:

Effective leaders are self-starters; they don't have to be asked to get the job done. They can get their fires burning without depending on external stimuli.

Humility. The last person you want to be around is the person who is full of himself. Billy Graham once said, "The smallest package in the world is a man all wrapped up in himself."

Emotional control. There is nothing wrong with blowing off steam once in a while. It's the loss of control that ruins the impact of many potential great leaders.

Humor. Humor attracts people, and making others laugh a little is a definite asset.

Positive attitude. People are attracted to positive people. Who wants to follow someone who's always in a foul mood or is always thinking doom and gloom? Instead, in a dark and negative world, the positive leader shines and draws others to him- or herself.

There are two types of people in the world. One is a leader, the other a follower. The difference received in compensation by each is vast. Only you can decide which type of person you will be.

. . . .

The real leader has no need to lead—he is
content to point the way.

—HENRY MILLER

It's hard to lead a cavalry charge if you think
you look funny on a horse.

. . . .

MANAGEMENT

We Are Two People

There is a psychological truism that all effective managers in business and industry have a firm grip upon. They understand this truism in depth, which is why they are so effective. It is a concept most people find very difficult to grasp:

We are all two people.

First, we are the person we present to those around us. This is the superficial facade we believe best represents what others want to see, and is largely a mirrorlike reflection of those about us.

Second, we are our real selves . . . who we keep safely locked away from the scrutiny of others, and quite often, from ourselves. Ideally, in the person who reaches total maturity and fulfillment, this dichotomy disappears. The person becomes unified, totally one person inside and out. For this person, the war is over; he or she has achieved peace within him- or herself and is totally free.

This is perhaps the goal that all effective managers, consciously or unconsciously, strive toward. They endeavor to lead each person to this ultimate end, thereby helping to develop a more productive personality.

Knowing that with the great majority of people, this inner self, this inner true identity, bears little relationship to the external facade that is presented to the world—understanding that this inner, protected person is soft, tender, sensitive, and extremely vulnerable, particularly to suggestions calculated to remove the real fears that dwell in the mind of the person they are managing—the knowledgeable manager plays on these sensitive fears as upon a harp.

The effective manager, or parent, often leads the person to completely remove or partially remove some of the fears that represent blocks to fulfillment, peace of mind, and a more successful, productive person.

Yes, most of us are two people, and the effective manager understands how to lead the two of us into one productive being.

. . . .

> Self-reverence, self-knowledge, self-control;
> these three alone lead one to sovereign power.
>
> —ALFRED LORD TENNYSON

Be that self which one truly is.

. . . .

MENTORS

The Golden Thread

Many years ago, I made a very interesting observation that has proved to be very beneficial. The world's most powerful, successful, service-oriented individuals frequently quote others who had gone down in history as having made a difference. Kennedy would quote Lincoln, or Churchill would quote Aristotle.

As I observed and thought about this golden thread that ran through their lives, I realized to quote leaders of the past, they must have studied what these leaders had said or done.

They were attempting to learn something from advice that was offered by great men and women who had proved they knew what they were talking about. Because I had a desire to emulate many of these achievers, I began to study their lives and the advice they gave us.

If you are not doing this now, you might try it.

During the Second World War, General Patton studied the life and philosophy of his opponent, Field Marshal Rommel, who commanded enemy forces. It paid off for Patton. He defeated his opponent, better known as the Desert Fox.

Every one of the giants had taken the advice of Harry Emerson Fosdick, who said, "No horse gets anywhere until it is harnessed. No steam or gas ever drives anything until it is confined. No Niagara is ever turned into light and power until it is channeled. And, no life ever grows great until it is focused, dedicated, and disciplined."

Mentally play with that quote for a while and you will learn something. Internalize Fosdick's advice and act on it, and you will realize just how effective you can become. You certainly will not go down in history as an also-ran.

Try it and see what happens!

. . . .

If thou art a man, admire those who attempt
great things, even though they fail.

In nature we never see anything isolated, but everything
in connection with something else which is before
it, beside it, under it and over it.

. . . .

THE MIND

The Magnificent Machine

I want you to imagine that you own the most magnificent automobile ever built. By some stroke of magic you never had to touch the vehicle. It was in a constant state of perfect performance. It was housed in a dustfree environment and the only time you ever used this prize possession was once every week when you drove it to the corner store to do your shopping.

Ridiculous, to be sure . . . however, we have something far more valuable. Yet, for some strange reason, the only use most people ever give it could be compared to the infrequent use of the automobile I just mentioned.

It is our brain. The organizer, the controller, the information-processing center of our body. Though it makes up only 2 percent of our body's weight, it hogs 20 percent of the blood supply.

It seems to take care of itself without any assistance from us. It eats first; that is, it takes its share of nutrients from the blood regardless of what has to go elsewhere. In case of malnutrition, the brain is the last to starve. It is the most powerful electrical instrument that has ever evolved.

Dr. Norman Vincent Peale, who was in charge of data processing for one of America's largest corporations, once told me that what is coming over the next decade will make anything we have today in data processing look primitive. However, he then explained that what is coming is a toy compared to your brain.

He was right on both counts.

You can use your brain to think, to build ideas, to solve any problem. You can use it to literally transform your life. It is there, finely tuned, self-maintained, all ready to drive you wherever you choose to go.

And when you gain an understanding of the inner workings of your conscious mind and subconscious mind, you'll really tap into your power and see your brain as a toy compared to your Mind. Your brain is an electronic switching station; it is an instrument of the Mind.

Mind is the greatest power in all creation.

. . . .

The empires of the future are the empires of the mind.

All the breaks you need in life wait within your imagination.
Imagination is the workshop of your mind, capable of
turning mind energy into accomplishment and wealth.

The mind is not a vessel to be filled but a fire to be kindled.

. . . .

MONEY

Become a Millionaire

How would you like to become a millionaire? That should bring a smile to your face. If you are like most people, you're secretly thinking, "Sure I would—that would be really nice. But I would have to win the lottery to do it."

Well, winning the lottery is one way of becoming a millionaire, but the odds stacked against you are pretty ridiculous.

You could cut those odds way down if you decided to earn a million.

In North America alone there are thousands of men and women who become millionaires every year. Every one of these new millionaires started out with the self-image of a millionaire before they became one. They actually saw themselves as millionaires.

You don't have to take my word for this. Study the millionaires you know. If you don't know any, and there is a large group of people who fall into that category, study the biographies and autobiographies of men and women who are millionaires. You will soon realize they never gained membership into this select club by accident. They consciously made a serious decision to become a millionaire.

Try this: Put a million in figures at the top of a sheet of paper, then break it up into smaller parts. The idea will start becoming more acceptable. Then get another sheet of paper and write down all of the ways you could make it happen.

I'll bet you a million dollars you are lot sharper than many people who have already earned a million. What's the difference between you and them?

They decided to do it.

Start playing around with the idea and you are going to realize fairly quickly that a million dollars is not that much money.

Money is better than poverty, if only for financial reasons.

Don't Let Wealth Escape You

*The good life is expensive. There is another way to live
that doesn't cost as much, but it isn't any good.*

The good life does cost a lot of money in today's fast-moving, materialistic world, but don't let that discourage you, because you can most certainly enjoy the good life if you really want to.

Make a definite decision to make some important changes in your life, and remember . . . money will definitely make your life more comfortable.

It is unfortunate, but not uncommon, to hear poor but well-meaning people say that money is not important to them; they just want to do good in this life.

In 1910 Wallace D. Wattles wrote *The Science of Getting Rich*. Wattles's reply to such statements was, "If you want to do good, get rich first."

Wattles was right. The good you can do without money will be limited to your physical presence at any given time. However, when you have an abundance of money, you are able to provide service to others in places far beyond your own physical presence.

Regardless of what your present financial position may be, realize that you can have money, all you want, but you must earn it. The great majority of our population lives in ignorance of this fact.

If wealth is something that has escaped you up to this point in your life, you are not unusual. Wealth has escaped the majority of people. What would be unusual would be your decision to do something about it. The library or good bookstores have excellent books that explain the basic fundamentals for a life of great wealth and unlimited service. Attend seminars that teach "how to earn more money."

When you make this decision, refuse to permit anyone to dissuade you.

It is not the creation of wealth that is wrong,
but the love of money for its own sake.

—MARGARET THATCHER

Give, give, give—what is the point of having experience,
knowledge or talent if I don't give it away? Of having
stories if I don't tell them to others? Of having wealth
if I don't share it? I don't intend to be cremated with
any of it! It is in giving that I connect with others,
with the world and with the divine.

—ISABEL ALLENDE

MOTIVATION

Trophies, Plaques, and Certificates

In almost every home or office you enter you will find a trophy, plaque, or certificate in recognition of some achievement.

These awards can play an important role in a person's life. They are great reminders that we can do work worthy of recognition. They can also provide the fuel that fires up our engines and can encourage us to continue on to greater achievements and personal growth.

These trophies can and will serve these purposes if we choose to let them.

On the other hand, we could make the terrible error of resting on our laurels, patting ourselves on the back, and talking about the good old days when we were making it happen—while all the while, our creative abilities are shut down, not getting the exercise they need for us to continually produce in an award-winning way.

While it is true that we do not need plaques or trophies to confirm how well we can or are doing, they can serve a purpose. Positive reinforcement is good for us.

It would probably be a good idea for all of us to check our wall of achievement. Make a mental note of the date on our last award. Become aware of what we are presently doing. It is very easy to slip into a rut of conformity and just move along at the speed of the masses.

These awards definitely serve as a source of renewal in one's life. They can also trigger fond memories in the autumn of our lives.

It is the time between the first and the last award where the game of life is played. Make your next performance another award-winning one.

Correction does much, but encouragement does more.

—JOHANN WOLFGANG VON GOETHE

I consider my ability to arouse enthusiasm among men the greatest asset I possess. The way to develop the best that is in a man is by appreciation and encouragement.

—CHARLES SCHWAB

Confidence . . . thrives on honesty, on honor, on the sacredness of obligations, on faithful protection and on unselfish performance. Without them it cannot live.

—FRANKLIN D. ROOSEVELT

Your Cheering Squad

Recently, I was speaking with a young lady who was knee-deep in various personal development programs. Her life was rapidly changing, inside and out. She was seeking advice on how to handle a particular problem and felt her situation was unique.

After listening to her, I knew exactly where she was going, as I had been there myself some years ago. I quickly assured her that her situation was quite common.

Almost all people who have set out to deliberately improve the quality of their lives are confronted with the same dilemma.

She found that when the going got tough and she was most in need of a cheering squad, she was faced with enemy troops.

You may be wondering what that means. Let me tell you.

When people begin to put their newfound positive ways into action and make some longed-for changes, they often find that something is amiss with the people in their lives. They begin to realize that some of the significant people, friends and family alike, don't seem to like the changes they are making.

What's even stranger is that these are the same people who say they want what's best for you. Yet they want you to stay just where you are . . . even if where you are as a person is a complete and absolute wreck.

Why?

Quite simple: The people in this young lady's life had been accustomed to interacting with her in a certain way. This interaction was based on who she used to be. Now that she has changed, the interaction must change and the people around her resist the change.

This, of course, causes conflict.

Many of the people she thought were friends and on whom she counted to help her chart a new course in life suddenly became enemy troops. And if that wasn't bad enough, not only did she find herself fighting her old internal habits, she also had to battle those around her.

If you find yourself in this position, do what I suggested she do: Keep going! Your cheering squad may be just around the corner. You will find people like you who want to better themselves and who are willing to help you improve and grow. You will ultimately attract a more positive, more supportive group of people into your life and you will win.

. . . .

It is not so much our friends' help that helps us,
as the confidence of their help.

—EPICURUS

. . . .

OBSTACLES

The Obstacle Course

*Obstacles are something everyone encounters in life.
The trick of a successful life is to conquer the obstacles
as they appear.*

I can vividly remember doing my basic training in the navy many years ago. We would get hauled out of bed at a ridiculous hour and marched in the cold to an obstacle course.

I was very young at the time and never understood what the navy was doing or why they were doing it. At the time it appeared to me as if my government had hired people who had a sadistic streak in their personality, and paid them to design these obstacle courses.

I honestly believed they were trying to kill us.

Looking back today, hopefully much wiser and certainly much richer from those experiences, I realize that they were trying to toughen us up, make men out of boys. The obstacles were causing my peers and me to get in touch with something within us we didn't even know was there. There is something else of real value I can see today that I totally missed years ago. Although there was always a certain amount of hostility felt by everyone prior to these marches, it was an enthusiastic group that returned—tired, but enthused. We had accomplished something; we conquered the obstacles. The leaders we referred to as sadistic prior to the march suddenly turned into good guys when we returned victorious. They were the same people with whom we were laughing and joking.

If you are in the middle of what appears to be an obstacle course today, reach out to meet the obstacles. Conquer them, and I guarantee that you will see yourself as a stronger, wiser, and happier person.

The marvelous richness of human experience would lose something of rewarding joy if there were no limitations to overcome. The hilltop hour would not be half so wonderful if there were no dark valleys to traverse.

I have learned that success is to be measured not so much by the position that one has reached in life as by the obstacles which he has had to overcome while trying to succeed.

—BOOKER T. WASHINGTON

Action is character.

OPPORTUNITY

For the Next Thirty Days

George Bernard Shaw once said, "People are always blaming circumstances for what they are; I don't believe in circumstances. The people who get on in this world are the people who get up and look for the circumstances they want and if they can't find them, they make them."

I want to suggest that beginning today for the next thirty days, you attempt to take control over your circumstances.

Millions of people are missing golden opportunities every day because they permit circumstances to stop them from accomplishing what they must accomplish to get what they want.

Whenever you find yourself saying or thinking, "I would like to do this or that but I can't, because . . ." understand that whatever follows the "because" is a circumstance, and the moment you say those words, you have given circumstance control over you.

The other day I was speaking with the executive officer in charge of a well-known sales organization. He explained that they were 15 percent behind quota for the year. When I asked him what they were going to do to make up for the shortfall, he quickly replied they would not be able to. He then began justifying his position.

Shun Fujimoto, a Japanese gymnast with a fractured leg in a plastic cast from his hip to his toe, was a gold medal winner at the Olympics in Montreal. He would not permit circumstances to keep him from realizing his dream.

In the 1950s there was good reason why you could not fit a powerful computer in a briefcase. Someone would not accept that idea—today you can carry a computer in a briefcase.

High achievers make things happen because they will not permit circumstances to stop them.

The important achievement of *Apollo* was demonstrating
that humanity is not forever chained to this planet
and our visions go rather further than that
and our opportunities are unlimited.

—NEIL ARMSTRONG

Once you make a decision, the universe
conspires to make it happen.

Man is not the creature of circumstances, circumstances
are the creatures of men. We are free agents,
and man is more powerful than matter.

Look Where You Are

"Greener pastures" is a phrase most of us pick up and think about fairly early in life. I would suggest, however, that the person who understands the real truth about greener pastures is a rare individual.

Hope seems to spring eternal in all human beings that the opportunities are greater elsewhere.

I suspect this uniquely human attribute or frailty has been at the root of all discovery. You must admit, though, that it is rather sad that many people spend so much time thinking of other pastures that they never properly appraise their own.

While we are looking at what the other person is doing and wishing we were in their pasture, others are wishing they were in ours.

I frequently have people tell me they wish they were doing what I am doing. Looking back in my own life, I clearly remember climbing the fence out of my pasture because the other person's opportunity was so enticing. By the time I had climbed back in again, my little excursion had cost me quite a few thousand dollars and a badly bruised ego. Somehow, succeeding always looks easier in the other person's line of work.

I'm not suggesting we should never make a change. Often, a complete change can be healthy.

But, before we do, we should take a long and careful look at what we are presently doing. Napoleon Hill said that we should not go searching for opportunity but reach out and embrace it right where we are.

Chances are, what you're doing is loaded with opportunities that someone else will benefit from if you don't. With the experience you already have, you can build a stairway to just about anything you want. "Want" is the key word!

You are, at this moment, standing right in the middle of your own "acres of diamonds."

Small opportunities are often the beginning of great enterprises.

Could we change our attitude, we should not only see life differently, but life itself would come to be different.

Two Brushstrokes

"The Chinese use two brush strokes to write the word 'crisis.' One brush stroke stands for danger, the other for opportunity. In a crisis, be aware of the danger, but recognize the opportunity."

Among other things, crises represent opportunities to grow in wisdom. When you approach each crisis with this attitude, you will pluck the opportunity out of each situation and benefit from it. This attitude also sets the stage mentally for you to continue to grow.

Everyone has problems, and the real producers have crises. And when they do, they search for the opportunity with wisdom and mental strength. Many great leaders aren't born with these qualities but they develop them if they weren't. The important element is how you handle crises.

Most public personalities must be mental giants. Their lives are examined and openly criticized frequently. For many people, this would be an unbearable crisis. However, to the personality that has high goals and a strong desire to reach them, the public criticism is viewed as unpleasant but a necessary part of the experience they require.

A diamond in its original state is a rough piece of coal. It is only through abrasion that it becomes a beautiful gem.

"Crisis": two brushstrokes. One stands for danger, the other for opportunity. Be aware of danger, but recognize the opportunity.

Excellent advice. Don't shy away from crises. You will become a stronger person.

. . . .

Opportunity often comes disguised in the form
of misfortune, or temporary defeat.

—NAPOLEON HILL

It is courage, courage, courage, that raises the blood
of life to crimson splendor. Live bravely and
present a brave front to adversity.

If opportunity doesn't knock, build a door.

. . . .

PARADIGMS

Change That Software!

Ninety-some percent of the population keeps getting the same results, year in, year out.

This is as true for students in school as it is for the person in business. If there is an improvement in the performance of most people, it's generally minimal— just a blip on the screen and not enough to make any substantial difference in a person's lifestyle.

Is there a problem? An enormous problem! It's called paradigms.

Paradigms can be likened to a program that has been installed in your brain. But you can change that software!

The same infinite power flows to and through each one of us, and if we had been taught to develop our higher faculties in the first place, we would understand how and why all things are possible.

You are going to be delighted to learn that just changing a very small part of the old paradigm can make an enormous difference in the results you can enjoy in every area of your life.

Think of the areas in your life that money affects. Imagine shifting your paradigm there to substantially increase your income before year's end.

If you have difficulty meeting people and you alter the paradigm so that it's easy and enjoyable to meet people, this could have quite an impact on your life.

These are just two examples of hundreds that could be done in YOUR life. Today!

There will be no permanent change in your life until the paradigm has been changed.

Choose one or two limiting ideas that are part of your paradigm and replace them with ideas that represent freedom to you. Consciously keep those new thoughts in your head, and act as if those thoughts are already imbedded in the foundation of your life.

Before you know it, your life will begin to change—and dramatically!

. . . .

We shall require a substantially new manner
of thinking if mankind is to survive.

. . . .

PERSISTENCE

The Only Difference

In Napoleon Hill's classic book Think and Grow Rich, *an entire chapter is devoted to persistence.*

Hill said, "There may be no heroic connotation to the word 'persistence,' but persistence is to character what carbon is to steel."

Think for a moment about any accomplishment in your past and you will realize that persistence played an important role in your success.

Napoleon Hill studied many of the world's most successful people. He pointed out the only quality he could find in Henry Ford or Thomas Edison that he could not find in everyone else was persistence. These men were often misunderstood to be ruthless or cold-blooded.

This misconception grew out of their habit of following through in all of their plans with persistence.

Milt Campbell was a friend of mine; we shared many hours together. Milt went to the Olympic Games in Helsinki, Finland, as a decathlon competitor. He was after the gold. Unfortunately, the man who had taken home the gold four years earlier in London wasn't satisfied with one gold; Bob Mathius wanted two. Milt had to settle for silver.

However, Milt had formed the habit of persistence, and four years later in Melbourne, Australia, he earned the gold.

On numerous occasions Milt said, "There were many guys in school who were far better athletes than me, but they quit."

I have studied successful people for over a quarter of a century and I'm convinced that the only difference between you and Edison, Ford, Campbell, or any other achiever is persistence.

What do you dream of doing with your life? Do it. Begin right now and never quit. There is greatness in you. Let it out. Be persistent.

Success is stumbling from failure to failure
with no loss of enthusiasm.

—WINSTON CHURCHILL

The best way out is always through.

Life shrinks or expands in proportion to one's courage.

Poor Start, Good Finish

There are literally thousands of men and women who are living dull, meaningless lives because they were not good students in school. They got poor grades, their report cards indicating that they were miserable failures.

Unfortunately, they permitted those poor grades to register as a part of their self-image and they still see themselves as failures years later.

These people never attempt to get a good job or an interesting position in any dynamic organization. They never attempt to start their own company, then build it into something of real value, because of this failure image they hold.

If you can relate to what I am saying, listen up, because I recently read a story of a man who was a poor student. You're probably familiar with his name. In fact, his name might be welded to the hood of your automobile.

He got poor grades in school but he never let it upset him, because he said his universe revolved elsewhere—around engines, motors, and bicycles. He was not only a poor student, he was a frail boy who did not do well in sports and suffered miserably from humiliation. The inferiority complex he developed was reversed and turned into a fierce desire to succeed . . . which he did.

Here are five personal principles for success this man used:

- Always be ambitious and youthful.
- Respect sound theories, find new ideas, and devote time to improving production.
- Take pleasure in your work and try to make working conditions as pleasant as possible.
- Constantly look for a smooth, harmonious working rhythm.
- Always keep in mind the value of research and hard work.

Most of the successful people I know got off to a poor start. If you did as well, don't let it stop you.

By the way, every time a Honda passes, you let it remind you of this story. That was his name.

. . . .

Nothing in this world can take the place of persistence.
Talent will not: nothing is more common than
unsuccessful men with talent. Genius will not:
unrewarded genius is almost a proverb. Education will not:
the world is full of educated derelicts. Persistence
and determination alone are omnipotent.

Failure is unimportant. It takes courage
to make a fool of yourself.

. . . .

PERSONAL POWER

Remove the Resistance

*It is not uncommon to hear, "Life sure is strange"...
and it is. Life is not something you can see, hear, smell,
taste, or touch. Life is something you experience; something expressed to a greater or lesser degree with one
person or another.*

What you and I refer to as life is really an invisible power that flows
to and through us. Our lives can be expressed in a very shallow,
bland manner or it can be vibrant and enthusiastic.

The invisible power we refer to as life operates in much the same
manner as electricity. No one knows what electricity is; we simply
have a little knowledge of what it does.

There is a law in electricity called Ohm's Law. Among other
things, it states that the amount of current that will flow in an electrical circuit will always be inversely proportional to the resistance
in the circuit. In other words, the less resistance, the more current
that will flow; the more resistance, the less current. Not only can
you increase or decrease the flow of electricity, you can use it for
destructive or constructive means.

That's also true with the power referred to as "life."

You are an instrument through which the life power flows. Resistance will limit the flow. You have many names for resistance—"doubt," "denial," "fear," "worry"—which will dramatically limit the flow of life through you.

Remove the resistance and this power has the ability to make an entirely new person out of you. This life power responds in some strange way to your beliefs, your mental attitudes, and your expectancies.

Look around. You see very little life flowing in some, and others who are radiant with life. Remove the resistance and live.

Destiny is no matter of chance. It is a matter of choice. It is not a thing to be waited for, it is a thing to be achieved.

PERSPECTIVE

The Gods-Eye View

This piece was written at 37,000 feet above the beautiful state of Kentucky. I was traveling to Toronto from Nashville doing something I frequently do when I'm traveling—I was looking down, quietly thinking of how different everything looks from up here.

Suddenly, I remembered a magnificent story I had heard years ago on a motivational record. It was a story that was very much in harmony with my present thoughts.

The author was referring to a poem written by Don Blanding called "The Gods-Eye View." Apparently, Blanding wrote the poem while he was flying as well.

The speaker on the motivational record made reference to an ancient Persian proverb about a bug in a rug and related the Gods-Eye View to a bug's-eye view.

If the bug could have raised itself above the Persian rug, he would have seen that what he considered enormous problems were actually something beautiful, something finely woven. Had he raised himself even higher, he would have seen that the finely woven tuft was a necessary part of a truly magnificent pattern.

As I looked down on Kentucky, this story slipped across my mind. I have thought many times that we live so much like the bug in the rug, pushing and shoving from one problem to the next in search of crumbs, complaining about life and how tough it is as we go through our days.

If we could relax and objectively raise ourselves above our problems, something the poor bug isn't mentally capable of doing, we would see our life from a completely different perspective.

If you happen to become overwhelmed today, a little uptight, the cause of your problem is probably the bug's-eye view.

Relax, and mentally switch on the Gods-Eye View. See how magnificent life really is.

I believe everyone should have a broad picture of how the universe operates and our place in it. It is a basic human desire. And it also puts our worries in perspective.

—STEPHEN HAWKING

Every man takes the limits of his own field of vision for the limits of the world.

If the doors of perception were cleansed everything would appear to man as it is, infinite.

—WILLIAM BLAKE

POSITIVE THINKING

It Can Go Right

Every time I hear Murphy's Law, I think of how negative it is: "If something can go wrong, it will." What a depressing way to look at life, and yet, unfortunately, that law is at work in the lives of many.

Wouldn't it be nice if there were some way we could prevent that law of Murphy's from affecting us? Well, there is, and I have found it.

Make up your mind to use the flip side of the coin—the opposite of Murphy's Law. Everything has an opposite and here it is:

"If something can go RIGHT, it will."

I'm going to call that Proctor's Law. Now the trick is to figure out how to get this beauty working in our lives.

And I figured that out, too.

If you study the writings of a great German literary giant, Johann Wolfgang von Goethe, you will find the answer. I quote:

"The moment one definitely commits oneself, then Providence moves too. All sorts of things occur to help one that would never otherwise have occurred. A whole stream of events ensues from the decision, raising in one's favor all manner of unforeseen incidents and meetings and material assistance, which no one could have dreamed would come their way."

I suppose in all fairness, we should call the positive side Goethe's Law: "If something can go right it will." He also cautioned us when he said, "Until one is committed, there is hesitancy, the chance to draw back, always ineffectiveness."

If you're a student, commit yourself to being an honor student. If you're in sales, commit yourself to a record month. Whatever you're doing, go all out. Set a goal to go to the top. Get committed and get lucky.

And remember: If something can go right, it will.

. . . .

Chaos is inherent in all compounded things.
Strive on with diligence.

There is no chance, no destiny, no fate that can circumvent
or hinder or control the firm resolve of a determined soul.

. . . .

The Law of Opposites

*Have you ever paid any attention to the idea that there
are two sides to everything?*

Look at your hand. It has a front and a back side. Your body has a right and a left side. The automobile or room you are in has an inside and an outside. You couldn't possibly have one without the other.

This is an orderly universe, of which you are a part. The whole universe is governed by laws.

The late Dr. Wernher von Braun said the natural laws of the universe are so precise that we do not have any difficulty today building a spaceship, sending a person to the moon, and timing the landing with the precision of a fraction of a second.

The law I am referring to is the law of polarity, or the law of opposites. If it is a long way up to the top of a building, it must be a long way down. If it is a mile from point A to point B, it must be a mile from point B to point A.

They are not only opposite; they are equal and opposite.

Everything that happens in your life today will appear either negative or positive. Keep in mind that whatever happens must have a positive side to it.

A large majority of the population seems to be mentally programmed to pay attention to the negative side of life and, unfortunately, to ignore the positive.

Make a decision right now that, regardless of what happens today, you are going to look for the positive aspect of what's happening. Remember . . . every cloud has a silver lining. Do this again tomorrow and the next day until it becomes a habit to see the positive in everything.

You will feel better. You will be more productive. You will have more friends.

> There is nothing either good or bad
> but thinking makes it so.
>
> —WILLIAM SHAKESPEARE

POTENTIAL

Don't Waste It

William James lived over one hundred years ago. He was a great student and teacher of human behavior. Most of what James taught then is true today. He suggested that, compared to what we ought to be, we are making use of only a small part of our physical and mental resources.

Stating this concept broadly, the human individual thus lives far within his limits. He possesses powers of various sorts that he habitually fails to use.

Years later, Thomas Edison, who demonstrated that we have tremendous potential, said, "If we all did the things we are capable of doing, we would literally astound ourselves."

When William James and Thomas Edison lived, information like that was scarce, relative to today's world. There was an excuse for people to live in ignorance of the truth about the potential we all possess.

That was then.

Today, self-help books top the bestseller lists. Audio programs and seminars on human potential are readily available in every town and city. Your automobile can instantly be turned into a learning center. By making a simple decision and a modest investment, the greatest minds of the past are available to you.

You can literally learn how to turn your wildest dreams into reality.

You can develop the mental stamina to persist and move toward your goals in the face of obvious disaster.

There is no need for anyone to permit the economy to be an excuse for failing.

Put this valuable information to use and recognize the greatness that exists within you. You have limitless resources of potential and ability waiting to be developed. Start today—there's never any time better than the present.

Be all that you are capable of being.

Always dream and shoot higher than you know you can do.
Do not bother just to be better than your contemporaries
or predecessors. Try to be better than yourself.

—WILLIAM FAULKNER

I dwell in possibility.

—EMILY DICKINSON

I have an almost complete disregard of precedent,
and a faith in the possibility of something better.
It irritates me to be told how things have always been done.
I defy the tyranny of precedent. I go for anything
new that might improve the past.

—CLARA BARTON

Not Too Late

*Do you feel it's too late for a new beginning . . . that
either you or the world won't be around for very long
anyway?*

*If you're still here, it is never too late. It is earlier than
you think.*

We're just beginning.

Our existence here on planet Earth to date can be measured as a
simple tick of the second hand on the clock of time. We have only
just begun to find out anything at all about the universe and our
place in it.

Charles Kettering, who invented the electrical switch for your
automobile, said, "We are just at the beginning of progress in every
field of human endeavor."

I suppose no age thought of itself as primitive. It considered itself,
at the time, as modern and up to date—whether it was the cave-
man era or the Gay Nineties. So it is understandable that we have
difficulty in grasping the truth that we, too, in many ways, are quite
primitive.

Future ages will look back on us . . . what we have and what we
are . . . in just the same way we look back on the days of the Roaring
Twenties or the Caesars. Our modes of transportation will be just as
obsolete as the Stanley Steamer.

But most incredible of all to future generations will be the way human beings of our time treated one another, and the almost complete disregard we had for the potential that lay dormant within us.

You have the potential for greatness.

You are quite capable of being or doing anything you can visualize. It is not your age, sex, race, or previous life experiences that will determine your future. It's the decisions you make. And it's never too late to begin something great.

Consult not your fears but your hopes and your dreams.
Think not about your frustrations, but about your
unfulfilled potential. Concern yourself not with
what you tried and failed in, but with what
it is still possible for you to do.

—POPE JOHN XXIII

Trust yourself. Create the kind of self that you will
be happy to live with all your life. Make the most
of yourself by fanning the tiny, inner sparks of
possibility into flames of achievement.

There are more things in Heaven and Earth . . .
than are dreamt of in your philosophy.

—WILLIAM SHAKESPEARE

PREPARATION

Preparation Is Everything

It was J. B. Matthews who wrote, "Unless a person has trained him or herself for their chance, the chance will only make them look ridiculous. A great occasion is worth to a person exactly what their preparation enables them to make of it."

Any winner will be quick to tell you that preparation is the key to success in any endeavor. You should make up your mind to become so good, so competent at what you are doing, you will actually force opportunities to come your way.

Take a serious look at your industry and ask yourself where you think your industry will be insofar as growth is concerned over the next ten years. If you can see no limit to the growth of your industry, then it is only reasonable to say there is no limit to your own opportunity for growth within your industry in the same time frame.

There are people in your industry who can write their own ticket. They have developed something inside that expressed itself through their behavior. It is called confidence. They are affecting life in their industry, rather than just being affected by it. They take thirty minutes or so every day to think of how they can put more into their job, how to be more creative, to provide a greater service.

Rather than just giving their time, they give all they've got.

In a period of five years or less, you can become an acknowledged expert in your particular industry. Surveys indicate that the great majority of people look at their job as being as far as they will go. They should realize that an expanding, dynamic industry not only needs but seeks the uncommon person to share in its growth, and will richly reward the person of vision and action.

Give everything you've got for the next ninety days. In return, your industry will give you everything you want for the rest of your life.

. . . .

We are what we repeatedly do. Excellence,
then, is not an act, but a habit.

Try, try, try, and keep on trying is the rule that must
be followed to become an expert in anything.

Quality is never an accident. It is always
the result of intelligent effort.

. . . .

PROBLEM SOLVING

Running into a Dead End

It is not uncommon to hear a person say, "I would rather be anywhere but here." Being someplace else has an aura of peace about it, a ring of hope, even a hint of new beginnings.

The lure of places that are new and addresses that are different entices one to believe things will be different.

Dealing with who we are and where we are causes us to wonder, from time to time, if escaping wouldn't be the best course of action. Some run away because they are afraid; others are afraid because they run away.

There would appear to be numerous enticements to run away. It must be easier somewhere else: the pay must be higher; the hours must be shorter; the weather would be milder; the people will be nicer; the cost of living is lower. The problems "over there" cannot match what I am facing here. The opportunities for advancement, happiness, and freedom are unlimited in that other environment.

Things will be different when I get there; the burden of here will be removed.

If you are even thinking that way, consider this: your zip code and area code might change, but one constant remains—you take your head with you.

Getting away is only positive when it is getting you closer to solving your problem. Run if running is your only option, but run inside toward your solution. Big doors swing on small hinges. The key to opening the door that will solve your problems is hidden where only you can reach for it.

Find out who you really are and become who you are destined to become. It may be a risk, but it beats running into dead ends while escaping.

- -

We cannot solve our problems with the same thinking
we used when we created them.

All the problems of the world could be settled easily if men
were only willing to think. The trouble is that men very
often resort to all sorts of devices in order not to think,
because thinking is such hard work.

We are continually faced by great opportunities brilliantly
disguised as insoluble problems.

- -

PROFESSIONALISM

What Makes a Pro

Watching any professionals perform is one of the most satisfying experiences in life. It makes no difference what the professionals are doing; they fascinate you with their skill and precision.

Years ago, I was employed by the fire department. I had a captain, Harry Taylor—we called him Scotty. I suppose by today's standards he would not be considered very "professional." Scotty never attended the fire college, but by my standards, he will always be a professional.

Some of the other officers who did attend the fire college and left with high marks had no idea of how to lead people. Scotty was a leader; he knew how to draw the best out of his people.

He was a pro.

Watch professional ice skaters. They leave you with your heart in your mouth as they go into some of their jumps, and yet they land with ease. You would almost believe they were born with skates on their feet.

Watch professional secretaries. They move with the same calm and assurance that the gold medal skater does.

Professional salespeople are poetry in motion. They go through their presentation calm and confident, overcoming objections, and leave with the order. And you never even heard them close the sale.

Professionals are a joy to watch. How do they become so good— or should I say, great?

They do little things in a great way every day. They work toward being at their very best, regardless. They know that amateurs compete with other people, but professionals compete with themselves. They study, practice, simulate every move, every day, many times. They want to be better today than they were yesterday.

Self-improvement is the name of the game, and
your primary objective is to strengthen yourself,
not to destroy an opponent.

As human beings, our greatness lies not so much
in being able to remake the world . . . as in
being able to remake ourselves.

PROGRESS

The Unreasonable Person

"The reasonable man adapts himself to the world: the unreasonable one persists in trying to adapt the world to himself. Therefore all progress depends on the unreasonable man."

That is a quotation from George Bernard Shaw's writings. If we were to paraphrase what Shaw wrote, I suppose we could say that people are considered reasonable when they are content with the way things are presently. However, when we encounter people who are dissatisfied with the status quo and endeavor to change it, they are frequently considered to be unreasonable.

This concept takes me back to a time when I was a young boy. My grandmother played an important role in my upbringing. She was continually telling me that I should be satisfied with what I had.

My grandmother was a real Angel of God in my mind, but as I look back to those days, I realize that there were a number of points she attempted to sell me where she was wrong. This was one of those points.

There is absolutely nothing wrong with being dissatisfied. In fact, there is a lot of good to be derived from a mind that is dissatisfied.

It was dissatisfaction that caused Edison to light up the world; Ford to give us the automobile; the Wright brothers to introduce us to a new kingdom; and Bell to enable us to speak to someone on the other side of the globe. All of these great advances were brought to us because their inventors were, as many believed, unreasonable.

The beautiful truth is that these inventors were dissatisfied.

If you are disagreeing with a present situation just to disagree, you are very likely unreasonable. However, if you are diligently attempting to improve a situation, absolutely refuse to permit someone else's remark that you are unreasonable to dissuade you. Be unreasonable in their mind, but move ahead.

In the long haul, they will very likely follow you.

Discontent is the first necessity of progress.

"Status quo," you know, is Latin for "The mess we're in."

PUBLIC SPEAKING

How to Give a Good Speech

Have you ever sat in an audience while someone has delivered a speech? I'm sure you have. The speech that was given without a typed-out script has almost always caught your attention and held your interest much faster and better than the one that had to be read.

I am not suggesting that you should not prepare, nor am I suggesting that you should not write your speech prior to delivering it. A good speech requires a lot of preparation. Here is a simple but very effective method of delivering a speech that I have used for years:

Know what you are talking about. You must be very familiar with your topic.

Write your entire speech, then polish it up and attempt to mix in a bit of humor. When you have the speech written, read it carefully, realizing that you have a picture painted in words. In fact, that is what a book is—a picture painted in words.

Next, divide the speech into a number of parts, each part a particular picture. Mentally visualize the various pictures. When you think, think in pictures.

Number the pictures. Take the first picture and mentally place it on your front doorstep. Put the second picture just inside your front door, the third picture in your living room, the fourth on the dining room table, and so on.

Sounds ridiculous, doesn't it? That's why it works. Memory is developed through ridiculous association. Now you're ready. When you step up front to give your dynamic talk, relax. Don't worry about what your audience thinks of you. It is none of your business what they think of you—just think about them. Mentally walk up to your house, open the front door, and, as your stroll through your home, describe the pictures you have mentally placed around the house for your audience.

Try it—it works!

If you make yourself understood,
you're always speaking well.

Fortune favors the prepared mind.

RELATIONSHIPS

The Best Gift

Since time began, we have been told by the wise that giving is much more beneficial than receiving.

There have probably been many occasions on which you had a good reason to question that advice, but even in those moments, your higher self would probably have agreed with the concept.

I came across something in a file I keep that suggests there is something you can give every day . . . something that would provide you with great compensation.

It costs nothing but creates much.

It enriches those who receive without impoverishing those who give.

It happens in a flash, and the memory of it sometimes lasts forever.

None are so rich that they can get along without it, and none are so poor but are richer for its benefits. It creates happiness in the home, fosters goodwill in a business, and is the countersign of friends.

Your gift will provide rest for the weary, daylight to the discouraged, sunshine to the sad, and nature's best antidote for trouble.

Yet, it cannot be bought, begged, borrowed, or stolen, for it is something that is no earthly good to anybody until it is given away! And, if it ever happens that a salesperson should be too tired to give one of these to you, you may want to give them one of yours.

For nobody needs one of these so much as those who have none left to give.

This is a bit of a riddle, isn't it? What on earth could provide so much for so little?

A SMILE. That's right, a smile!

Make up your mind to give a big one to every person you come in contact with today. A smile . . . from ear to ear. And pay particular attention to the reaction you get from every person you give one to.

. . . .

A warm smile is the universal language of kindness.

A tree is known by its fruit; a man by his deeds. A good
deed is never lost; he who sows courtesy reaps friendship,
and he who plants kindness gathers love.

The level of our success is limited only by our imagination
and no act of kindness, however small, is ever wasted.

. . . .

Use Their Name

Here is a simple little test you can try for the next twenty-four hours to get and hold a person's attention. If you are pleased with the results of your test, I would encourage you to keep doing it until it becomes a habit.

Lead off whatever you have to say, to everyone you speak with, using the person's name.

It has been recognized since the time of Plato and Socrates that most people consider their name to be the most beautiful sound in the world, and they will pay more attention to sentences in which it appears.

Giving a person a compliment using their name is a way of showing that the compliment you give is tailored uniquely to fit that person.

For example: "Sue, your hairstyle is very attractive. It really highlights your face." Or, "John, your shoes are really sharp. They go well with your suit."

Another interesting point about using a person's name is that it causes a greater level of interest in the conversation and, most important, the listener will listen intently to the statement following their name to see how well it will relate to them. Each time you make an important point, preface it with the listener's name. The attention given to your opinion and its retention will greatly increase.

Become a name-user, not a name-dropper. There is quite a difference. When you become a name-user, others will remember you and what you have to say for a longer time.

When you first meet a person, listen closely for their name. If it is a difficult name to pronounce, you might politely ask the person to spell it for you. This will help you to remember their name.

Once you've got it—use it effectively.

. . . .

People will forget what you said, people will forget what you
did, but people will never forget how you made them feel.

. . . .

RISK

Safe and Sorry

When you were growing up, how often did you hear the words "It's better to be safe than sorry"? Probably too often, especially when you became aware that most people who played it safe ended up sorry.

It is the risk takers who generally end up winners!

How many people do you know who have passed up a magnificent opportunity because they might have had to mortgage their house or quit the job they had held for a number of years?

Rather than step out boldly, they stepped back into safety.

Abraham Maslow said, "You will either step forward into growth or step back into safety." He also advised us that if you plan on being anything less than you are capable of being, you will probably be unhappy all the days of your life.

I am not suggesting that you become irresponsible, which is quite different from taking risks, although I will agree it is a fine line that separates the two.

The opposite of taking a risk is, of course, playing it safe. The latter would probably be a reasonable way of life for seventy or eighty years—if you had a contract to live for a thousand years. Playing it safe is a pretty dull way to live, and you end up looking back on your life wondering what would have happened if you had done this or tried that.

People who play it safe are generally not very exciting. In fact, they would probably border on being very boring.

On a scale of one to ten as a risk taker, where do you stand?

Add a little spice to your life today and take a risk. Remember, if you play it safe you may end up sorry.

Only those who dare to fail greatly can ever achieve greatly.

—ROBERT KENNEDY

Power is given only to those who dare to lower
themselves and pick it up. Only one thing matters,
one thing; to be able to dare!

I'm not afraid of storms, for I'm learning to sail my ship.

—LOUISA MAY ALCOTT

SALES

So You're a Salesperson

When you stepped into the sales arena, you entered the most complex and fascinating profession in the entire world. Selling offers the lowest and highest incomes of all professions. It is either a depressing existence or a fulfilling, creative adventure.

Selling, as a profession, accepts every applicant regardless of their past history, age, sex, race, religion, or formal education. It rejects no one. As a profession, it has no prejudices. When it comes to rewards, the sales profession is like Aladdin's lamp. The world is yours for the asking.

There is, however, one prerequisite to enjoy the many rewards selling offers: YOU MUST SELL.

It is possibly the only profession that requires every one of its members to pass a test many times every day, and there are no graduates, ever. You must spend a part of every day developing yourself—intellectually, spiritually, and physically. The salesperson who is not involved in such a daily program very quickly becomes a brake on the wheel of progress.

This type of deliberate personal development properly prepares you to pass your daily tests in a calm, efficient manner. It will also qualify you to earn the tremendous rewards, both mental and material, that your profession offers.

Professional salespeople make commitments. Without commitments, you will be relegated to the rank of amateur, and as an amateur salesperson your days would be filled with little more than a host of disappointments.

By making a series of commitments and keeping them, you will be writing your own personal passport to prosperity and fulfillment.

. . . .

Everyone lives by selling something.

The quality of a person's life is in direct proportion
to their commitment to excellence, regardless
of their chosen field of endeavor.

—VINCE LOMBARDI

. . . .

Steamboat Salespeople

A wise man of the Orient once remarked, "There are three kinds of salespeople in every company: rowboat salespeople, sailboat salespeople, and steamboat salespeople."

Rowboat salespeople need to be pushed or shoved along. They generally start too late and quit too early. Because they are attempting to move ahead in the most strenuous manner, they take frequent breaks from their work and never seem to get very far. In their minds, because they seem to be working hard and investing a considerable amount of energy, they believe they are doing a good job.

The rowboat salespeople are almost always puzzled by their small paychecks.

The sailboat salespeople only move in the direction of their desired goal when a favorable wind is blowing. They leave their success entirely in the hands of circumstance or some other outside source. When the winds of the surface are blowing in their direction, they are all smiles and honestly believe they deserve the credit for their good fortune. Unfortunately, this misguided group generally ends up on some rocky shore, blaming nature for their failure.

These sailboat salespeople are equally puzzled by their sparse compensation.

The steamboat salespeople are in great demand and are well compensated. They move in the direction of their chosen destination continuously, through calm or storm. They are usually masters of themselves, their surroundings, and their fate.

Whenever they are slowed down or stopped from moving ahead, they are aware that the problem lies in the engine within. They immediately begin their necessary repairs. The steamboat salespeople know that neither the winds of the surface nor their physical strength is retarding their progress . . . it's inside. They solve the problem and move forward to fame and fortune.

Are you in sales? Start your engine and win!

Sales are contingent upon the attitude of the salesman—
not the attitude of the prospect.

Always bear in mind that your own resolution to
succeed is more important than any other.

—ABRAHAM LINCOLN

SELF-IMAGE

A New You

In today's world of self-help seminars, books, and audios, there is a lot of talk about self-talk. We have always talked to ourselves but, until recently, you very rarely heard people openly admit it. Talking to yourself was considered to be a sign of mental instability.

Not anymore. Now it's the "in" thing to do.

If you want to win, positive self-talk will keep you moving in the direction of your goal. Successful people generally think and feel positively about themselves. They translate these feelings and thoughts into powerful words and phrases, creating a stream of self-talk that helps them become or continue to be successful.

The positive self-talk then translates into the action that produces the results they desire.

Begin today to be your own best friend, your best supporter. When you talk to yourself, select words that describe your positive qualities and characteristics. Talk about the good, not the bad; the success, not the failure; the accomplishments of each day rather than what you did not complete; how you can as opposed to why you can't.

As you adopt and practice this process, and make it a daily ritual, you will begin to experience a new you.

The language you use in positive self-talk will create a new reality. Your perception of who you are and what your value is with respect to your business, your family, and your community will change in your mind. This chain of new positive thought introduces a different thought pattern. Ultimately, through daily practice of positive self-talk, you will achieve greater results.

You'll be amazed at how quickly you'll notice a much more vibrant you!

Nothing builds self-esteem and self-confidence
like accomplishment.

If you do not conquer self, you will be conquered by self.

Self-image sets the boundaries of individual accomplishment.

SELF-KNOWLEDGE

Try Visiting with Yourself

I'm writing this at 35,000 feet, somewhere between Tulsa, Oklahoma, and Atlanta, Georgia. In fact, I write quite a lot up here.

There is an empty seat beside me, it's a beautiful, smooth flight, and I am thoroughly enjoying this time alone. Just visiting with myself. Thinking of me . . . who I am . . . where I'm going . . . what I want to change to improve in my life.

Suddenly my mind flipped back to one day last week when I was attempting to pick a date to have dinner with a couple of new friends. There were three or four calendars involved and we got frustrated attempting to find a time when everyone was free. We finally decided to get back to each other this week; we never did set a date.

Sitting here on the plane alone, thinking about that telephone call and the dinner date, I realized just how busy everyone is, the speed we are moving at in our lives today. Then, all of a sudden, I realized why I rather enjoy being up here in any airplane. I'm alone, with nothing to do but visit with myself.

I believe it is important that we spend some time alone: no outside distractions, a time for a little introspection. The more time we spend with another person, the better we get to know them. The same is true of our self. Making time to visit our self is a good investment, something we can be richly rewarded for. We become more friendly toward our self and develop a deeper respect for our real potential as a creative being.

I am well aware that there are those who cannot tolerate being alone. They must be with someone or doing something constantly.

I lived a good part of my life like that. I never enjoyed being alone, because I did not enjoy my own company. I wasn't a very interesting companion, for me or anyone else—until I began to get in touch with my real potential.

If you are busy, on the move as I am, you might want to do what I have just decided to do. Schedule a little more time to visit with yourself. Find out how interesting you can be.

Thinking: the talking of the soul with itself.

Conversation enriches the understanding,
but solitude is the school of genius.

All men's miseries derive from not being
able to sit in a quiet room alone.

STUDY

There Is No Competition

A clear 90 percent of the population in North America reads at a grade-seven level. That's because we learn to read by the time we have reached grade seven and never improve our reading ability from that point on.

Shocking, isn't it?

It is not only shocking, it's a shame. But what is even worse is that this lack of personal development goes well beyond reading. Most people do whatever they do in much the same manner.

There are very few people who master anything.

Ask any sales executive and they will quickly agree that there are mighty few people who ever master selling. The same is true of managers, lawyers, accountants . . . I could go on.

There is really no competition in the marketplace. You'll have great masses in any profession out there making a noise. Those few souls who are actually studying their craft, attempting to perfect it, stand out in a crowd like a giraffe in a herd of field mice.

The masters in any profession can name their own price, write their own ticket. Yes, their stock is always high; their rewards are great. If you don't already belong to this small, select group of high achievers, I have good news. There is plenty of room in their club and it is not difficult to qualify.

Begin to study what you do for a short time every day, knowing that you can always perform better. Work toward a specific result well beyond your present level of performance.

Just one hour of concentrated study each day adds up to nine forty-hour weeks in one short year. Think of how much more you would know in five, ten, or twenty years.

I began doing this myself twenty-five years ago. Today, I receive more money for one hour of my time than what I was once paid annually. When I started to study, I learned this great secret of achievement.

Ignorance is the curse of God; knowledge is the
wing wherewith we fly to heaven.

—WILLIAM SHAKESPEARE

Every addition to true knowledge is an
addition to human power.

If a man empties his purse into his head, no one
can take it away from him. An investment in
knowledge always pays the best interest.

—BENJAMIN FRANKLIN

To Get What You Want

I've talked about you making a decision to alter the conditioning in your subconscious mind. I also mentioned that to accomplish this, you must study and exercise a respectable amount of discipline. Study and discipline are the prerequisite to any form of accomplishment.

Unfortunately, however, studying is much like paying taxes for most of us—we only do it when we have to.

What is the alternative? There has to be one. Well, there is, but for me it is not acceptable, and when you consider the alternative, I'm sure it won't be for you either.

The alternative to studying is that you must carry your ignorance with you wherever you go forevermore. You must not only carry your ignorance with you, you will advertise it to the entire world in your thoughts, feelings, and actions.

What are the rewards for studying? My friend, that is the yeast that raises the dough.

Yes, you can have whatever you want. The world is yours for the asking. But you must learn how to be, get, or do it—and learning requires study.

Remember the lyrics to the song "Welcome to My World"? "Knock and the door will open. / Seek and you will find. / Ask and you will be given / the key to this world of mine." You should study the esoteric meaning of the lyrics of that beautiful song. They are rich with truth.

The only two sources you can refer to if you want to study life are science and theology. They both tell us that nothing is created nor destroyed. Everything you want is here in one form or another.

To get what you want, you must learn how. To learn how, you must study.

. . . .

He who learns but does not think is lost! He who thinks
but does not learn is in great danger.

I am always doing that which I cannot do, in order
that I may learn how to do it.

. . . .

SUCCESS

Impossible to Fail

Have you ever wondered why so many honest people work hard and achieve so little, while others never seem to work hard and get everything they want? They seem to have that magic touch—everything they touch turns to gold.

People who fail have a tendency to continue to fail, while those who succeed go on from one success to another.

This obvious fact has puzzled the majority of people for centuries.

For half of my life I belonged to the large group who were puzzled. Then I was encouraged to study the lives of those who were on the success track. They seem to all live by the same philosophy. They think highly of themselves and have trained their minds to choose positive, effective ideas.

William Shakespeare put it this way: "Our doubts are traitors, and make us lose the good we oft might win by fearing to attempt."

One of the real jewels in my library is a book that was written many years ago by Dorothea Brande, titled *Wake Up and Live!* Her entire philosophy can be reduced to one powerful line:

"Act as tho' it were impossible to fail."

Imagine how your life would be if all of your decisions were guided by a concept like that! You can have the things you want—all of them. And you will have them if you begin to see yourself with them.

Think of what I have said and you will understand why some win and others lose.

Adopt Dorothea Brande's philosophy—it worked for her. Act as though it were impossible to fail.

. . . .

One's only rival is one's own potentialities. One's only failure is failing to live up to one's own possibilities.

We must dare to think "unthinkable" thoughts. We must learn to explore all the options and possibilities that confront us in a complex and rapidly changing world.

Our duty, as men and women, is to proceed as if limits to our ability did not exist. We are collaborators in creation.

. . . .

Need vs. Desire

I came across some notes on "Need vs. Desire." There is a difference—a big difference. Many people desire success, few need it. But those who do need it almost always enjoy it.

Needs are what you must have to survive. You need food, air to breathe, clothing, shelter, sleep, etc. What you need to survive you get at any cost.

When you convince yourself that you need success, just as you need to eat when you are hungry, it comes without you even having to think about it.

What is your definition of success? Attaining a certain income level? Learning a skill? Enjoying a certain lifestyle? Achieving a certain position in the company?

We all have different mental pictures of success, but few people ever totally achieve it. Why? Our mental picture of our self is not what it must be. Some wonder if this mental picture can be changed, and the answer is an emphatic yes!

To create a need, you must first set a goal. When the goal is placed before you, you employ self-motivational techniques. You make that goal a need. It becomes a driving force. You convince yourself that the goal must be reached in order for you to survive.

When you develop that state of mind, you will most definitely succeed.

If you were lost in a desert without water and saw a water hole some distance away, although you knew that a hard, painful effort was needed to reach it, the decision would be automatic. No degree of difficulty would stop you. However, if you had lots of water and thought a fresh drink would be nice, the degree of difficulty might well put you off.

Yes, there is a great difference between need and desire.

Desire is the key to motivation, but it's determination and commitment to an unrelenting pursuit of your goal—a commitment to excellence—that will enable you to attain the success you seek.

—MARIO ANDRETTI

Formula for success: rise early, work hard, strike oil.

The Power Within

Under ordinary circumstances the word "failure" has a very negative connotation. I would like to give this word new meaning because it has been very misused in the past.

The word "failure" has brought an untold amount of grief and hardship to millions of people.

First and foremost, it is important to distinguish between failure and temporary defeat.

Sir Edmund Hillary failed in the eyes of many people, in 1951 and again in 1952, in his attempt to climb Mount Everest. However, in Hillary's mind he had merely met with temporary defeat. No doubt they were disappointing and costly setbacks, but not failures, because in 1953, he and Tenzing Norgay, his Sherpa guide, were the first people to reach the 29,028-foot summit of Mount Everest.

Temporary defeats are often a blessing in disguise. They have a tendency to bring us up with a jerk and to cause us to redirect our energies along different and more desirable paths.

I have a theory that temporary defeat is nature's way of strengthening us and giving us the courage necessary to reach our goals. It takes a lot of courage to view temporary defeat as a blessing in disguise. No one ever got up from the knockout blow of defeat without being stronger and wiser from the experience. You can only be classified as a failure when you refuse to get up and go at it again.

Advancement of all kinds is generally preceded by a crisis. The greater the crisis, the greater the opportunity of advancement.

Eliminate the word "failure" from your vocabulary. You can always get up and go at it again tomorrow. There is no problem outside of you that is superior to the power within you.

A man can fail many times, but he isn't a failure
until he begins to blame somebody else.

Far better is it to dare mighty things, to win glorious
triumphs, even though checkered by failure . . . than
to rank with those poor spirits who neither enjoy
nor suffer much, because they live in a gray twilight
that knows not victory nor defeat.

—THEODORE ROOSEVELT

THINKING

The One Percent Difference

Many years ago I was attending a seminar that a good friend of mine, Leland Val Van de Wall, was conducting. He said something that broke me up; in fact, the entire audience roared with laughter. He said, "If most people said what they were thinking, they would be speechless."

A very wise man. He was correct as well.

A number of years ago, I had the pleasure of sharing the platform at a convention with the late Dr. Kenneth McFarland, a great educator from Kentucky. He said something similar.

Dr. McFarland said, "Two percent of the people think, three percent think they think, and ninety-five percent would rather die than think."

I recently read where George Bernard Shaw said, "Most people think two or three times a year. I've gained an international reputation for myself thinking just two or three times a week."

You're probably saying to yourself by now, "Come on, Bob, everyone thinks." Is that right? Well, let me suggest that you listen closely to most of the conversations going on around you over the next few hours. It will be obvious that most of those talking are not thinking, or they would never say what they are saying.

Watch the behavior of some of your peers. You will realize they are not thinking, or they would never do what they are doing.

You could fall into the 3 percent group, which Dr. MacFarland referred to as those who think they think.

With a little effort, you could catapult yourself into the 2 percent group that DOES think. They are the achievers; the winners in life.

Thinking must be learned, and it is a subject not taught in most schools. Think about it.

> Rarely do we find men who willingly engage in hard, solid thinking. There is an almost universal quest for easy answers and half-baked solutions. Nothing pains some people more than having to think.
>
> —MARTIN LUTHER KING JR.

> If everyone is thinking alike, then somebody isn't thinking.
>
> —GEORGE S. PATTON

> A great many people think they are thinking when they are merely rearranging their prejudices.

The Preamble to Everything

Your inductive reasoning factor: what a magnificent tool. This one gives you true freedom. Reason gives you the ability to choose your thoughts.

Viktor Frankl, the great Viennese psychiatrist who spent years in concentration camps during the Second World War, wrote in his book *Man's Search for Meaning* that, regardless of the physical or intellectual abuse he received from his captors, they could not make him think something he did not choose to think.

Thinking is the highest function you are capable of, and this mental faculty should be exercised at every possible opportunity. Thought is the preamble to everything in your life.

All of the great leaders down through history have told us we become what we think about. In fact, they have been in complete and unanimous agreement on this point, while they disagree on almost every other point.

Unfortunately, the vast majority of people rarely think. They simply accept what they see or hear.

The next time someone gives you a suggestion, rather than simply accepting and acting on it—THINK. Exercise your reasoning factor. Ask yourself if the suggestion will improve the quality of your life.

Here is another great exercise for your reasoning factor, one I am in the habit of using myself, which will give you almost anything you want:

Take a pad and pen. At the top of the pad, write down something you want but have not in the past given serious thought to accomplishing. Begin to think of how you can get what you want without violating the rights of others. Write off why you can't get what you want.

As simple as this exercise sounds, very few people do it. Most people think of what they don't want. As a result, they cheat themselves out of the good that life offers.

Think. Think deep, penetrating thoughts . . . and your reasoning factor will become strong.

More gold has been mined from the thoughts of
men than has been taken from the earth.

—NAPOLEON HILL

There are a thousand thoughts lying within a man that
he does not know till he takes up a pen to write.

Lulled in the countless chambers of the brain,
our thoughts are linked by many a hidden chain;
awake but one, and lo, what myriads rise!

The Silent Switch

We are gradually awakening to the fact that we live in a Universe of Infinite Intelligence that responds to our every thought, but only those who delve into the study of the mind really know what a mighty energy is set in motion with each mental impulse.

Thought not only molds our character but is responsible for the changes in communities, the building of cities, the shaping of nations, and all of the great events that take place in the world. THOUGHT IS THE SILENT SWITCH THAT SETS IN MOTION MAN'S DESTINY.

Every invention and worthwhile discovery was first a mental concept. Every idea that has been backed with faith and effort has become a visible reality, and all seeming material obstructions such as poverty or physical weaknesses have only served to stimulate creative action by giving birth to inward resources and bringing out inherent abilities.

About a year ago I spent some time with Rick Hansen. Rick is a young man who was left paralyzed from the waist down after an automobile accident. He told me that his physical disability turned into a good thing. Because his disability was physical, he could see it and overcome it. Although he was virtually unknown and without money, he pushed himself around the world in his wheelchair and raised millions of dollars for spinal cord research.

It was Rick Hansen's thoughts that liberated him from a dull, pitiful life. His thoughts gave him a life full of adventure, a life full of service to thousands, a life that caused millions of people to look at themselves and think of what they were doing with their lives.

Thought is a tremendous power, and you can use it to improve the quality of your life and the lives of others.

. . . .

Life always expresses the result of our dominant thoughts.

The day science begins to study non-physical phenomena,
it will make more progress in one decade than in
all the previous centuries of its existence.

. . . .

TIME

How Will You Spend It?

*Regardless of how you look at your stay here on this
Earth, you must admit that life is short. You and I
possess the potential to make out of our lives whatever
we choose.*

We all get the same amount of time every day . . .

We get all there is.

To waste any of the precious commodity we refer to as time is a disgusting thought to my mind. Unless I am extremely tired, I even resent the time I spend unconscious each night . . . or should I say, most nights. There are occasions when I do not sleep at night.

Now listen closely, because if you haven't yet figured this out, what I am about to say will hopefully shock you into a more exciting way of life.

The average person spends four hours each day in front of their television set. That adds up to ten and a half years between the ages of two and sixty-five. Add that to the twenty-one years that same average person spends sleeping, which is what eight hours a night works out to, and you will realize that exactly one half of the sixty-three years I am referring to is spent either totally unconscious or in front of a vacuum tube creating a head to match.

Think about it: thirty-one and a half years either in front of a TV or sleeping. This is not an indictment against TV, and I agree, we must rest, but this is ridiculous!

If you truly wanted to accomplish something in this life and you happen to fall into the category I am referring to, you know what to do. If you just cut back two hours a day in each of these two areas, you would add sixty twenty-four-hour days to each year.

That's a lot of time. You could enjoy a richer life. Over the sixty-three years I am referring to, you would have an extra ten years to accomplish whatever you choose.

That is a lot of time we will all spend. How are you going to spend it?

A man who dares to waste one hour of time
has not discovered the value of life.

Time is what we want most, but what we use worst.

VISION

Build the Picture

Many years ago, Helen Keller was asked if she thought there was anything worse than being blind. She quickly replied that there was something much worse. She said, "The most pathetic person in the world is a person who has their sight but no vision."

Any thinking person would quickly agree with Helen Keller.

When people have no vision of a better way of life, they have automatically shut themselves into a prison; they have limited themselves to a life without hope.

This frequently happens when people have seriously tried on a number of occasions to win, only to meet with failure time after time. Repeated failures can damage people's self-image and cause them to lose sight of their potential.

They give up and resign themselves to their fate.

Vernon Howard wrote that you cannot escape from a prison if you do not know that you are in one. Howard is right—these people are in a prison of their own making and don't know it. Without a vision of a better life, there can be no hope.

If you happen to be caught in this type of negative cycle, take the first step in predicting your own prosperous future. Build a mental picture of exactly how you would like to live. Hold on to that vision, and positive ways to improve everything will begin to flow into your mind.

Think of this: Your vision is a mental picture of the actual lifestyle of many people you either know or know of. Realize this simple truth. If they can do it, you most certainly can.

All people have the same potential to live their dream. It is simply a matter of utilizing the unlimited potential we all have.

A desire presupposes the possibility of action to achieve it;
action presupposes a goal which is worth achieving.

—AYN RAND

Deep into that darkness peering, long I stood there,
wondering, fearing, doubting, dreaming dreams
no mortal ever dared to dream before.

—EDGAR ALLAN POE

I imagine that yes is the only living thing.

—E. E. CUMMINGS

Quixote Attitude

Man of La Mancha was one of Broadway's most successful plays. In the play, Don Quixote is near death. He has been mocked and scorned because he is such a positive thinker.

Perhaps you can relate to how he must have felt.

Finally, in an excellent stand of self-defense, Don Quixote asks the ultimate question: "Who is crazy? Am I crazy because I see the world as it could become? Or is the world crazy because it only sees itself as it is?"

Don Quixote presents us with a tremendous question. Ask yourself: Who is crazy, the realist or the idealist? Bringing all of your conscious attention to bear on your present results will produce more of the same results, just as certain as the night follows the day.

This is why unhappy people tend to remain unhappy. It is why lonely people tend to remain lonely. It is also why poor people tend to remain poor.

James Allen wrote, "The visionaries are the saviors of the world"—and they are. All of the wonderful inventions that have made our lives more comfortable were brought to us by the Don Quixotes of the world. These individuals saw the world as it could become.

If you happen to get a little down today or you have been in a rut, develop the Quixote attitude. See your position at work or at business, your relationships, your marks at school, or your sales as they could become.

Build a beautiful picture of the improved results in your mind.

Don't permit the naysayers to sway you. Form the Quixote attitude and have fun. You'll be amazed at what you can accomplish.

Your vision will become clear only when you can look
into your own heart. Who looks inside, awakes.

—CARL JUNG

Without leaps of imagination, or dreaming,
we lose the excitement of possibilities.
Dreaming, after all, is a form of planning.

—GLORIA STEINEM

Remember always that you not only have the right to be
an individual, you have an obligation to be one.

—ELEANOR ROOSEVELT

WINNING

The Razor's Edge

It has often been said that the line that separates winning from losing is as fine as a razor's edge, and it is. I am referring to winning in a big way, in all areas of life.

Somerset Maugham wrote an entire book titled *The Razor's Edge*. Darryl Zanuck produced a movie with the same title. Both of these men knew there wasn't a big difference among people; there was only a big difference in the things they accomplished.

One person almost starts a project; the other person starts it. One individual almost completes a task; the other person does complete it. One student nearly passes an exam; the other person passes it. Although the difference in their marks may be only one percentage point, it's that one percentage point that makes all the difference.

In 1947, Armed was the highest-earning racehorse in the history of United States. That year, Armed had earnings of $761,500. Yet the horse that finished second in earnings that same year, a horse that often lost races a mile long by only a nose, won only $75,000.

If you were to look at the winnings alone, it would appear that

Armed was thirteen times better than his closest competitor. However, when you compare the times that were actually registered by these two horses in their races, you discover that Armed wasn't even 4 percent superior.

It's the little things you do that can make a big difference. What are you attempting to accomplish? What little thing can you do today that will make you more effective?

You are probably only one step away from greatness.

Whenever I go on a ride, I'm always thinking of what's
wrong with the thing and how it can be improved.

—WALT DISNEY

A winner never stops trying.

—TOM LANDRY

He that can heroically endure adversity will bear
prosperity with equal greatness of soul; for the
mind that cannot be dejected by the former is
not likely to be transported with the latter.

Rhythm and Winning

The tide goes out, the tide comes in. Summer follows winter. Night follows day. A bad economy is followed by a good economy. You laugh and you cry.

These are an expression of the law of rhythm—a law of the universe that affects everything and everyone.

Amateurs point to the low swing in the economy as the cause of their poor production. If the economy is the cause of poor production for one person in a particular industry, everyone in that industry would also have poor production. However, you know that is not so. In every economy—good and bad—some win and some lose.

There is a way to win, regardless of the economy. You're probably asking, "What is it?"

There are many ways to win. THINK and you will find them. You may not find all of them, but you will find enough answers to move you over with the winners.

I was speaking to a group the other day and I suggested that doing the same things you did when the economy was good is not good enough. You will have to put more coals on the fire in a poor economy to get the same heat you received in a good economy. You must give more energy, more thought, more service.

Listen to positive-thinking programs more frequently; refer to your inspirational books more often. Become more selective about whom you spend time with. Love a little more, hate a little less. When an associate begins complaining, change the subject to what's good or walk away.

Think about it. You don't have to ride that roller coaster. You can progressively move on an upward path toward any goal.

The choice is yours as to whom or what controls you!

Continuous effort—not strength or intelligence—
is the key to unlocking our potential.

Happiness lies in the joy of achievement and
the thrill of creative effort.

—FRANKLIN D. ROOSEVELT

Apply yourself both now and in the next life. Without effort,
you cannot be prosperous. Though the land be good, you
cannot have an abundant crop without cultivation.

WORK

Do What You Love

The humanistic psychologist Dr. Abraham Maslow devoted his life to studying self-actualized people: that tiny portion of the population who made the most of their human potential.

Maslow's research showed that these people had a number of things in common. Most important, they did work they felt was worthwhile and important. They found work a pleasure, and there was little distinction between work and play. Maslow said that to be self-actualized you must not only be doing work you consider to be important, but you must also do it well and enjoy it.

Maslow recorded that these superior performers had values, those qualities in their personalities they considered to be worthwhile and important. Their values were not imposed by society, parents, or other people in their lives.

Like their work, they chose and developed their values themselves.

These discoveries of Maslow are important if you want to get the best out of life. Do you have values? Did you choose these values yourself? Do you find your work worthwhile and important? Do you find your work a pleasure? Do you find that there is little distinction between your work and your play?

If you are not answering yes to these questions, perhaps you should seriously consider making a change.

Your life is important and, at its best, life is short—very short. The older you get, the more you will become aware of exactly how short and important life is. Changing jobs or letting go is a scary proposition even for a confident person. However, you must agree that the alternative is much worse.

You have the potential to do anything you choose, and to do it well. Today would be an excellent time to start.

There is no passion to be found playing small—in settling for a life that is less than the one you are capable of living.

—NELSON MANDELA

The Work's Never Completed

Have you ever noticed that you never seem to get your work completed? In fact, you shouldn't—if you are moving in the right direction.

The task you are presently working on should cause your business to become more successful, which, in time, creates more work or more business.

Apparently, there are individuals who do not seem to realize this basic truth. One such person was always harried, hurried, and explosive because of the amount of work he thought he had to do. This individual was told by a psychiatrist to plan to do only six hours of work in an eight-hour day and spend one day a week at the cemetery.

"What am I supposed to do in a cemetery?" asked the astonished victim of his own wrong thinking.

"Nothing much," said the psychiatrist. "Just look around, get acquainted with some of the people who are in there permanently. And remember that they didn't finish their work either. Nobody does, you know."

Pretty good advice, I'd say.

There is an amusing twist to the psychiatrist's suggestion, but it would certainly make even a slow-minded person think. Even the idea of planning to do only six hours of work in an eight-hour day could be wise advice for some people. I am familiar with many who do four hours' work in what should be an eight-hour day, although they might take ten hours to do it, because their minds are in a continual state of confusion.

My perception of the psychiatrist's advice is to quit rushing, work steady, and be effective. There is always tomorrow. If you plan to be effective and you have your priorities straight, you will complete the important tasks, and the others can wait.

The main point of the good doctor was right on the money: The graveyard is full of people who never got everything done.

Men for the sake of getting a living forget to live.

Work is not man's punishment. It is his reward
and his strength and his pleasure.

It is only when I am doing my work that I feel truly alive.

WORRY

The Psychic Disease

Worry is a psychic disease that has become a national pastime. You should also understand that it is more contagious than smallpox.

Worry causes you to become very lethargic and irritable—in other words, very poor company. Worry is the forerunner to fear, which causes anxiety and, ultimately, physical disease.

You will never, let me repeat, never witness any truly productive behavior expressed from a worrisome mind. You should not mistake worry for a conscious concern. There is a vast difference in the two.

You are worrying when you choose negative thoughts and direct them toward a particular end.

Permit me to give you an excellent example that is true.

A number of years ago I was living and working in Los Angeles. I had an occasion to be in Toronto and I was visiting a friend. He was in a very poor frame of mind, not at all a pleasant person to be around.

That wasn't too bad for me, I was just visiting. His family was in a much different position.

I asked his wife what the problem was and she explained he was worried sick because he was $2,000 short to meet his payroll the following week. I spoke to him and said a lot could happen in a week, don't worry. That didn't help. I took a checkbook from a Canadian bank and gave him a check for $2,000. I said, "If you don't use it, Don, give the check back to me when I return."

His personality changed instantly. He was happy.

The following month, Don returned the same check, saying he did not have to use it. I replied, "That's good, Don, because there was no money in that account."

Ninety-two percent of what you worry about never happens. Don't worry, be happy!

Every tomorrow has two handles. We can take hold of it with the handle of anxiety or the handle of faith.

Worry is the interest paid by those who borrow trouble.

I have learned over the years that when one's mind is made up, this diminishes fear; knowing what must be done does away with fear.

—ROSA PARKS